# BLACK SUNDAY

## The Great Dust Storm of
## April 14, 1935

## FRANK L. STALLINGS, JR.

EAKIN PRESS ⋆ Austin, Texas

Edited by Melissa Locke Roberts
Text design by Amber Stanfield

For CIP
information,
please access:
www.loc.gov

FIRST EDITION
Copyright © 2001
By Frank Stallings
Published in the United States of America
By Eakin Press
A Division of Sunbelt Media, Inc.
P.O. Drawer 90159 ☜ Austin, Texas 78709-0159
email: eakinpub@sig.net
💻 website: www.eakinpress.com 💻
ALL RIGHTS RESERVED.
1 2 3 4 5 6 7 8 9
**1-57168-528-6 PB**

*To the spirit of those whose*
*lives were forever imprinted*
*by the storm that turned a*
*Palm Sunday into Black Sunday.*

For Kate and Charlie —
Hope you don't feel too
dusty after reading
all this. Best wishes —
Fred Haley

*This photo was taken by Harry Eisenhard, photographer for Associated Press, who accompanied reporter Robert Geiger, on assignment from the Denver office to write about and photograph conditions in the Dust Bowl. As the two approached Boise City, Oklahoma, the April 14, 1935, storm was right behind them. They stopped, Eisenhard took the photo, and they hurried to get to Boise City so the picture could be developed and telegraphed to Denver, where it was published in the* Denver Post *the next day.*

— Courtesy AP/Wide World Photos.

# CONTENTS

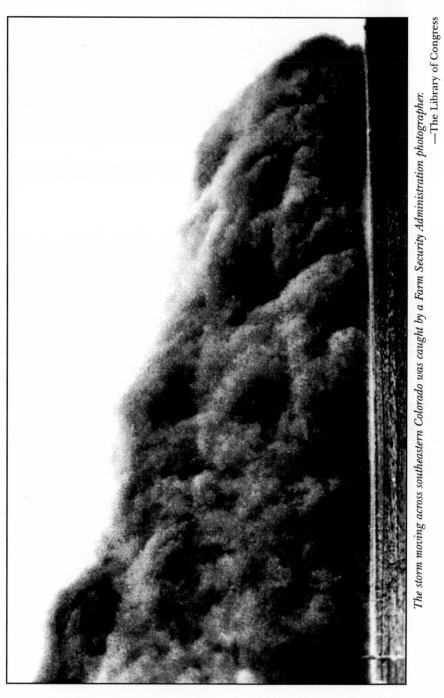

*The storm moving across southeastern Colorado was caught by a Farm Security Administration photographer.*

—The Library of Congress

# PREFACE

Preparing this book took more years than were in the original plan. After many interviews, letters, phone calls, visits to museums, and general gathering of pictures, anecdotes, and other materials, I thought, in 1984, that it would be a pleasant thing to have the book completed and published by 1985, the year of the semicentennial of the Black Sunday dust storm. Other things seemed intent on my failure to meet that deadline, partly because of a call to act as interim chair of the Literature and Language Department at Northern Kentucky University. After that interlude came health difficulties for me and my wife. Then it seemed that the huge mass of material I had collected was more than I could find a pattern for that would be interesting.

I never planned for the book to be a scholarly study, complete with all the paraphernalia of such works. I intended it as a collection of reminiscences, reports, and responses to the storm by individuals who had been in it, by newspapers that had covered it during April 1935, and by newspapers that revisited the event in subsequent years, especially 1985. It became apparent as time passed that there were specific events (the Tyrone rabbit hunt, for example) that were worth looking at separately. Finally, I discovered a number of other kinds of sources—poems, the one-act play "Dust," and several humorous anecdotes.

What resulted is a compilation I hope readers will find interesting. It tells the story of a single dust storm—among the hundreds that plagued the Dust Bowl in the 1930s—one giant, black storm that became the signature event of a devastating period in the history of the South Plains.

After all the interviews were recorded, transferred to computer, printed out, and filed, there were over 200 pages, most of them single-spaced. The stories are told by people from many walks of life, all of whom experienced the same event at the same time, remembered it, heard about it, told about it. Now others can hear the voices, perhaps, and feel the emotions that have caused this one rare natural disaster to remain a part of the history of individuals as well as of the geographical area where the storm occurred.

FRANK L. STALLINGS, JR.
Highland Heights, Kentucky
January 2001

# ACKNOWLEDGMENTS

As with any oral history, the number of people to whom an author (or editor, as it may be) owes a debt is enormous. Without the stories and reminiscences about the event that is the central subject, there would be no way to tell the story from so many points of view. The list of those interviewed, those who wrote, those who called, those who sent pictures and other kinds of materials that fill in otherwise blank places—that list is at the end of the acknowledgments.

Too, there are the people whose constant question has been (for almost two decades), "How is the book coming?" Finally, their desire that I complete the work has borne fruit, and their forbearance has been the cause of the weight on my heart that pushed me to do what should have been done long ago. Most especially due thanks for patience is Ethel Wilder Johnson, my aunt, whose eagerness to help with the original interviews, and who participated in many of the conversations, has been an enormous influence on the whole process from the beginning—in fact, even before this project was begun. Then there is Joe Stallings, a nephew whose interest in the story and whose kind questioning about when the story would be told kept me reminded that I had not completed what I started. My wife, Virginia, was from the start interested in what the people said about the Dust Bowl and the big storm because she never got to see a really big duster (though we encountered a small red one in western Oklahoma on our way through there some years ago) and has wondered what it was like to be in one. Perhaps her curiosity was as much a reason for my finally sitting down and putting this all together as was the personal feeling that, if I did not do it, I would be letting down scores of people who looked forward to seeing their words in print.

I was treated with the utmost respect everywhere I went during the search for those who had been present in the area of the Dust Bowl when the Black Sunday duster blanked out the sun instantly. Especially I have to thank Louise and Gaston Tribble of Liberal, Kansas, whose hospitality made it possible for me to interview dozens of people who had lived in and around that area since before the big storm. Louise, especially, asked people to come to the Liberal Public Library, where I had a tape recorder and enjoyed conversations for several days with old timers whose memories fill quite a number of pages of this study. Del Guidinger, then librarian at the Liberal Public Library, made certain that the interviewer and interviewees had a place to talk and provided me much information and sources from newspapers about the storm. Dr. Fred Rathjen, professor of history at West Texas State University (now West Texas A&M), was instrumental in pointing me to the large collection of materials dealing with the Dust Bowl in general and much about the Black Sunday storm. He and Betty, his wife, were hospitable hosts to me and Virginia during our stay in Canyon, and Fred introduced me to The Westerners, an organization that meets regularly and talks about historical matters dealing with the West, of course. Their discussion of Black Sunday was interesting and at times quite jovial.

At the Panhandle-Plains Historical Museum, Claire Kuehn helped immeasurably by showing me how to find materials dealing with dust storms and with the Dust Bowl in general. There is enough material in that archive to fill many volumes. At the No Man's Land Historical Museum in Goodwell, Oklahoma, Joan Kachel, manager, showed me a collection of pictures and other materials related to the storm. Jane Brite did the same at Miami, Texas, in the Roberts County (Texas) Museum. My thanks also goes to John Stevens, soundman at Northern Kentucky University, who transferred my cherished album of Woody Guthrie's *Dust Bowl Ballads* from scratchy 78 RPM records to a CD for me. Joe Ruh, Northern Kentucky University's photographer, spent many hours translating 35mm slides into publishable form.

When I stopped at newspaper offices, businesses, homes and museums, and met people in cafes and at get-togethers, everyone was eager to talk about the storm, of course, but also about the whole depression era in Kansas, Oklahoma, Texas, Colorado, and New Mexico. These folks gave me photos, newspaper articles, told jokes, helped me with copying documents, and generally wanted the story to be told lest it be forgotten.

Now I must thank the following individuals, some of whom I know have since passed away. Their comments remain here not only for historical value, but also for their families, who are too young to have known the vicissitudes of the 1930s. My appreciation for all those who contributed to this work is much more sincere than it would seem from the amount of time it took to make the book. I'm sure there are people who need to be listed but whose names do not appear on this list. For that I add sincere apologies.

The first city listed is the residence of the source in 1983 or 1984. The second city (in parentheses) is where the person was at the time of the storm in 1935, if different from first city. Page numbers reference a quote from that person.

Dr. Lewis Armstrong, Liberal, Kansas/p. 70
Theda Badmaieff, Fullerton, California (Beaver, Oklahoma)
Fanny Bailley, Miami, Texas/p. 34
James Bain, Clarendon, Texas
Ernest Baird, Pampa, Texas (Miami, Texas)/p. 52
Lawrence Balzer, Hooker, Oklahoma/p. 64
Gene and Erma Lee Barber, Pampa, Texas/p. 11
Dr. R. M. Bellamy, Pampa, Texas/pp. 51, 149
Jennie Rose Benton, no town listed in document where her
    comments appeared, Panhandle-Plains Historical Museum/p.
    27
Mrs. Eunice Bohot, Pampa, Texas/p. 25
Lois Boynton (Mrs. Hallie H.), Pampa, Texas/p. 13
Ruth Brooks (Mrs. Horace), White Deer, Texas/pp. 14, 85, 95
Maxine Browne (Mrs. Clifford), Liberal, Kansas (ranch in
    northern part of county)/pp. 19, 20, 72

Ruby Burke (Mrs. H. L.), Beaver, Oklahoma/p. 15
Mrs. Jenkie Campbell (Mrs. W. R.), Miami, Texas
Tracy Cary, Pampa, Texas/p. 106
Emery Chaffin, Liberal, Kansas
Paul Cherry, Tyrone, Oklahoma (photographer of the Tyrone rabbit run)
Mrs. Henrimae Christopher, Amarillo, Texas (document in Panhandle-Plains Historical Museum)/p. 36
Orville Christopher, Miami, Texas/p. 62
Hazel Clark (Mrs. J. F.), Pampa, Texas/p. 30
Bert Clifton, Dalhart, Texas
Fontaine Cooley, Guymon, Oklahoma (Moreland, Oklahoma)/p. 63
Betty Lou Collier, Fort Worth, Texas (Pampa, Texas)
Sammy Cope, Liberal, Kansas/p. 7
Anna Cox, Great Falls, Virginia (Pampa, Texas)
Leon Daugherty, Pampa, Texas (Hoover, Texas)/p. 44
Myrtle Davidson, Pampa, Texas (diary entry from Mrs. Davidson, grandmother of Fred Vanderberg, Sr.)/p. 27
Mrs. A. B. Davis, Jr., Lubbock, Texas/p. 36
Margaret Dial, Pampa, Texas
Ollie Dunivee, Miami, Texas/p. 62
Jim Dunn, Liberal, Kansas (Garden City, Kansas)/p. 54
Faye Eaton, Amarillo, Texas
Ben Ezell, Canadian, Texas (Quitaque, Texas)/p. 63
Bula Flynn, Pampa, Texas (Amarillo, Texas)/p. 33
Bill Foran, Canyon, Texas
Lyda Gilchriest, Pampa, Texas/p. 8
Maggie Gill (Mrs. Elmo), Miami, Texas (Laketon, Texas)/p. 28
Jessie Glynn, Dumas, Texas
Mr. and Mrs. Fred Godwin, Pampa, Texas (Lefors, Texas)
Bob Gordon, Pampa, Texas (Mobeetie, Texas)/p. 61
Joe Gordon, Pampa, Texas
Mildred Grider (Mrs. R.C.), Pampa, Texas
R. C. Grider, Pampa, Texas/p. 44
Sylvia Grider, College Station, Texas
William S. "Bill" Griggs, Canyon, Texas
Ben Guill, Pampa, Texas/pp. 42, 141
Mary Frances Guinn, Pampa, Texas

James Lambuth Hague, Dallas, Oregon (Tyrone, Oklahoma, rabbit drive)/p. 73
Carl Hare, Canyon, Texas
Mr. and Mrs. Lee Harrah, Pampa, Texas/p. 12
Sherman Harriman, Boy's Ranch, Texas/p. 59
Maxine Hawkins, Pampa, Texas/p. 12
Ivey Hickey (Mrs. Joe), Liberal, Kansas (farm between Meade and Plains, Kansas)
Bob Hill, Beaver, Oklahoma/p. 20
Mildred Hill, Beaver, Oklahoma/p. 20
Clyde (Bud) Hodges, Miami, Texas (Canadian, Texas)/p. 67
Harold Hudson, Perryton, Texas/pp. 63, 110
Bill Hutchinson, Lake Charles, Louisiana (Pampa, Texas)/p. 64
Jean Jenkins (Mrs. Harmon), Lubbock, Texas (Floydada, Texas)/p. 10
Blanch Jenkins, Miami, Texas/p. 34
Ethel Johnson, Pampa, Texas/pp. 3, 37
Eleanor Keesling, Liberal, Kansas (Guymon, Oklahoma)
Irene Kennedy (Mrs. Robert L.), Liberal, Kansas/p. 19
Hugh Kilgore, Hooker, Oklahoma
Clarence Kinkaid, Lubbock, Texas/p. 10
James S. Kone, Amarillo, Texas/p. 59
P. Claude Ledrick, no address
Dale and Frieda Lewis, Pampa, Texas (en route from Sayre to Lawton, Oklahoma)
Charles Light, Liberal, Kansas
Travis Lively, Jr., Pampa, Texas
Travis Lively, Sr., Pampa, Texas (Lefors, Texas)/p. 45
Ellis Locke, Miami, Texas
Charles and Jan Lockhart, Miami, Texas
Dr. Ruth Lowes, Canyon, Texas
Ruth L. Lowray, McLean, Texas (Pampa, Texas)/p. 36
Helen Ruth Mackie, Pampa, Texas (Eli, Texas)/pp. 10, 24
Jesse Mays, Pampa, Texas/p. 47
John McCarty, Amarillo, Texas (Dalhart, Texas)/p. 84
Willie McClary (Mrs. Jack), Dumas, Texas/p. 29
Mrs. Roger (Willie) McConnell, Pampa, Texas/p. 13
Mrs. J. M. McCracken, Pampa, Texas/p. 38
Dyke McMurry, Dumas, Texas

Eleanor McNamara (Mrs. Andrew), Pampa, Texas (ten miles south of town)/p. 29

Margaret Morgan (Mrs. J.M.), Tulsa, Oklahoma (southwest of Pampa, Texas)/p. 38

Buff Morris, Canyon, Texas (Friona, Texas)

Lillian Mullinax, Pampa, Texas

Russell (Rusty) Neef, Pampa, Texas (oil lease between Pampa and Borger, Texas)/p. 61

Edwin Nelson, Pampa, Texas (Hereford, Texas)/p. 62

Harry Nelson, Sr., Pampa, Texas

Don Nicholson, White Deer, Texas

Jack Osborne, Pampa, Texas (Perryton, Texas)/p. 62

Thelma Paris, Miami, Texas/p. 34

Richard Parsley, White Deer, Texas

Phyllis Perkins, Bryan, Texas (Pampa, in 1936)

Cloie Phillips, Dumas, Texas

Woody and Juanita Pond, Miami, Texas (Pampa, Texas)/p. 27

Byron Price, Canyon, Texas (Curator, Panhandle-Plains Historical Museum)

Howard Qualls, Dumas, Texas (McLean, Texas)

Anna Reed, Great Falls, Virginia (Pampa, Texas)/p. 34

Phoebe Osborne Reynolds, Pampa, Texas (between Plainview and Miami, Texas)/p. 28

Mrs. Kathryn Rowley, Hooker, Oklahoma (Turpin, Oklahoma)

Gerdes Schmidt, Miami, Texas

Donna Belle Schultz (Mrs. W.H.), Liberal, Kansas/p. 22

Alma Seitz (Mrs. Charles), Miami, Texas/p. 31

Elva Jean Shepic, Canyon, Texas/p. 29

Joe and Charles Shelton (father and son), Pampa, Texas (driving from Oklahoma)/p. 40

Ralph Sloan, Pampa, Texas (in Oklahoma that day)

Dean Smith, Liberal, Kansas (hitchhiking, Shawnee to Beaver, Oklahoma)/p. 43

Irl and Irene Smith, Pampa, Texas (Groom, Texas) (photographs)

Noel Southern, Pampa, Texas (Tyrone, Oklahoma, rabbit run)/p. 69

Mr. and Mrs. Dudley Steele, Pampa, Texas (in Lefors that day)/p. 49

Mr. and Mrs. Bruce Stevens (Betty), no address
Avanelle Milligan Stone, Waco, Texas (White Deer, Texas)/p. 31
Faye Stowell, Pampa, Texas (Gruver, Texas)/p. 64
Per Stubbe (Mrs. Martin), Pampa, Texas (south of Shamrock, Texas)/p. 26
Joe Taylor, Canyon, Texas
Dorothy Teed, Topeka, Kansas (Pampa, Texas)
O. B. Thomas, Amarillo, Texas
Clotille Thompson (Mrs. Fred), Pampa, Texas
Maidee Thompson, Pampa, Texas (Buffalo Flat, Texas)/p. 24
Robert Tucker, Liberal, Kansas
Fred Vanderberg, Sr., Pampa, Texas/p. 55
Winifred (Wimpy) Vaughn, Broken Arrow, Oklahoma (Pampa, Texas)
Frances Walls, Pampa, Texas (Miami, Texas)/p. 8
Mr. and Mrs. Delmer Webb, Liberal, Kansas (Tyrone, Oklahoma, rabbit run)/p. 72
Wilbur Wells, Guymon, Oklahoma/p. 63
Sylvia Wesendonk, Lubbock, Texas/p. 35
Mr. and Mrs. William Wilder (Hortense), Akron, Ohio (Lubbock, Texas)/p. 35
Betty Fisher Williams (Mrs. Paul), Liberal, Kansas/pp. 16, 70
Bonnie Williamson, Miami, Texas /p. 28
Mr. and Mrs. George Winchell, Balko, Oklahoma (Tyrone, Oklahoma, rabbit run)
Charles Woodburn, Amarillo, Texas
Earl Young, Dumas, Texas (between Vega and Umbarger, Texas)

*"Dust Clouds Rolling Over the Prairie"* needs little more said.

—Stovall Studio Photo, Dodge City, Kansas

# INTRODUCTION

The Dust Bowl of the 1930s was partly the result of indiscriminate plowing of Great Plains grasslands from the end of the nineteenth century into the 1920s and using the land to raise wheat, other grains, and feed for livestock. The settlers who began the process were not aware that their plows would make the land blow away in the 1930s, when a combination of drought and wind blew uncovered soil from one place to another in storms that eventually gave rise to the term "Dust Bowl."

During the years when dust blew and topsoil-stripped farmlands were unable to grow much of anything, some people pulled up stakes and moved to California or other places where there were no dust storms. Such people became known as "Okies" (even though most were from places other than Oklahoma). They would be remembered in legend and song and *The Grapes of Wrath*, John Steinbeck's classic story of the Joads.

Even though some left the area, most people stayed where they were, survived as best they could, cursed the dust, and prayed for rain while constantly being harassed by winds that blew dust and by dust that crept into every niche and crevice of their houses. They became accustomed to the dust, as much as possible. Between 1933 and 1938, dust storms, especially in the spring, were so common that there was even a kind of resignation that it would be over "someday," and that staying where they were would be the only way to survive.

On April 14, 1935, an incredible dust storm rolled across the Dust Bowl area. The date would become—as have the anniversary dates of Pearl Harbor, the death of President Kennedy, the end of World War II—memorable to the extent that people

1

in that region still like to recall exactly where they were and what they were doing and pass on that experience to following generations.

Variously called Black Sunday, Black Easter (wrongly, because it was actually Palm Sunday), "the granddaddy of 'em all" and "that thing" (oddly clear to those who watched its coming and then witnessed its blackness), this dust storm is pictured in hundreds of photographs kept by families as if to make sure everyone knows what it was like to go through "the end of the world" and live to talk about it.

As the following reminiscences, newspaper reports, and afterthoughts show, this storm was not like other storms—it was sudden, enormous, black, and it "rolled" over the land. It turned a sunny, warm, relatively windless Sunday into a nightmare for many, an adventure for some, a natural phenomenon never to be forgotten by almost everyone who was there. "There" is an area of eastern Colorado, southwestern Kansas, the Oklahoma and Texas panhandles, and northeastern New Mexico. The storm had traveled from its origin in South Dakota, gathering more and blacker dirt as a north wind pressed it southward, and then was pushed into the core of the Dust Bowl area, where it became the monster that rolled across the region, instantaneously turning sunshine into midnight. That much almost everyone agrees upon. But as with all memorable events after the passage of time and the retelling of the stories by parents to children and then to grandchildren, variations in their telling emerge: Did the wind nearly knock people down when the dust hit? How long did it remain so dark "you couldn't see your hand in front of your face"? What happened as a result of the storm—anything different from the usual activities of a Monday morning after a dust storm?

In the 1970s I began to collect materials about Black Sunday by talking to my parents and aunts and uncles who had been in the Texas Panhandle during the storm. My only two distinct memories of this dust storm were that my father, Frank L. Stallings, Sr., and I were out in the vacant lot on the north side of our home in Pampa, Texas, flying a kite on that bright Sunday afternoon. I was seven years old at the time. Flying a kite was fun, especially the feel of holding the kite as it pulled its way upward in the breeze, which I recall that day was blowing in from the south. My father looked toward the north, saw a black line across the horizon, and said we had better start reeling in the kite. I do not remember feeling any sense of danger because I have no recollection of anything else about the storm until we were in the house and I was standing at one of the front windows. Then I remember seeing two Chinese elm trees in the front yard bending over almost parallel to the ground. I do not remember darkness, except that we (my two brothers and I) seemed to be told to go to bed earlier than normal, and it was dark at that time. I recall nothing of what happened the next day. I probably went to school (first grade) at Horace Mann, but I don't even remember that.

My lack of memory, however, was not typical of the many who were adults at the time. Sometime in 1971 I put on tape some things that occurred to me about the storm, not all of which are accurate, as it turns out. I said, "It seems to me that it was in the very early spring of 1936, but I don't know for sure." I said, also, that "I do remember that the next morning our house was literally an indoor dust pile." Actually I do not remember that. It was obviously something I picked up from someone telling me about the next day. Nor do I remember the incident my Aunt Ethel Wilder Johnson (fourteen years old at the time) told about her father (Dr. H. L. Wilder), my father, and my Uncle Henry Wilder going outside the house to see the storm and coming back into the house minutes later covered with black dirt. It is likely that much of the lore about the Black Sunday storm has come down to us after all these years in the form of stories heard from grandparents, parents, and other elders.

In 1983 and 1984, I made a concerted effort to find people who were in the area on that day and record their recollections of the storm. The stories in this book are taken from tapes and notes of the conversations we had, as well as from letters sent by those whom I missed. Some generalizations can be made from the material collected from those who told me their stories.

Houses, at least most of the houses occupied by those I talked with, were not built to keep out dust when it was blown by winds of thirty miles an hour or more. The dirt being blown was more like flour than ordinary soil (probably ground that fine by having been blown over many miles). Most houses had wooden window frames and sashes that had shrunk over the years from drought (even in the best years, rain was on average eighteen inches or less), and almost all windows and doors were without any sort of weatherstripping. Dust could also come in under doors, around loose window panes, and so much into attics that they had to be shoveled out occasionally to keep the ceilings from collapsing. Many farm houses in those times still had no electricity, no running water, no indoor plumbing.

Automobiles and passengers in them were also victims of dust. Most cars at the time had no air filters, which meant that dust could penetrate into engines and wear out parts in record time. The dry air, combined with the constant wind across the plains, created static electricity that frequently stalled cars and made necessary such "improvements" as wires and chains that dragged the ground to prevent shocks when a person touched a metal part. Like houses, cars lacked tightness, so dust could come in through the cracks around the windows and doors, even when closed.

Farm implements took the same beating as did cars, except that they were frequently called upon to work while dust was blowing—often stirring up enough dust themselves to create a small storm on a windy day. Farm implements left out in open fields too long faced the probability of being buried under drifts of dirt, as many pictures show. Fences, especially barbed-wire fences used to keep farm animals in, were often used in the worst storms as guides to lead someone to a barn or a house. The wire was often a carrier of static that could shock the unwary or the ungloved. After blowing tumbleweeds collected against a fence, dust drifts in the weeds often got high enough that cattle could walk over the fence.

Except for major highways between cities, roads to almost everywhere were unpaved. These roads became quagmires in wet times, but during droughts and dusty periods, the ditches filled with tumbleweeds that caught dust and became traps for cars that ran off the road. During the Black Sunday storm, most roads were useless because the storm canceled out car lights, and drivers would have to depend on seeing fencelines or ditches in order to find the way. At the darkest time of the storm, no light penetrated, and the driver had to stop until enough light came through for the trip to continue. Several people recalled driving fast enough to outrun the storm, which traveled (depending on the teller) at fifty miles per hour or more.

This dust storm interrupted every activity people engaged in that Sunday afternoon: church services became prayer vigils; weddings were not completed; burials had to be postponed until the next day; picnics, swimming parties, and rides (the Sunday ride was then a common family recreation) turned into flights for home; airplane flights had to be shortened or canceled; farm activities such as milking had to be abandoned (or the milk thrown out because of the dirt in it); children had to be sought, even when nearby, as the blackness made them disappear; cooking became impossible until the dust had settled. Perhaps the most famous among activities interrupted by the dust storm was a rabbit run near Tyrone, Oklahoma. A hundred or more people gathered in a field and many more stood watching while rabbits were driven toward a fence where they were to be slaughtered, loaded on trucks, and carried to the state prison or taken home for supper. Just as the run was at its climax, the storm hit and blacked out everything. All but a few rabbits escaped. At least a dozen of my sources mentioned that rabbit hunt, and many of them had copies of a picture taken at the time.

Besides the stories taken directly from tapes recorded or letters received during the early 1980s, I have used newspaper accounts of the storm, supplied by individuals who saved them. But since the dust storm has survived in so many ways, I have included later accounts from newspapers discussing reminiscences thirty or fifty years later, especially fifty years after the storm. Inevitably there is a great deal of repetition among the stories about the storm, but in spite of that, the words and ways of telling the stories are all individual and thus different.

The Black Sunday duster did not do the kind of damage that a flood or earthquake or hurricane or tornado would do. It only laid down a thick layer of dust that was difficult to remove because it was so fine it clung to surfaces, and in some accounts it was described as being oily enough to adhere to inside and outside walls. But it was terrifying because day became night instantly. Ironically, some called it beautiful because it was huge enough to create a kind of awe mixed with terror. It was also the kind of event that remains in the memory because in the midst of an almost intolerable depression and drought, this was thought to be the final straw, perhaps "the end of the world."

It was not the end of the world, of course, because the preachers insisted that though the end of the world might come in a cloud, surely it would not come in a dust cloud. It was not even the end of the dust, which remained a threat to the Dust Bowl region for at least another five years after 1935. In the 1950s, another drought brought fears of another Black Sunday, and in the 1980s another depression and drought revived such talk. The most significant result of the big black duster was that it would be the storm to which all later storms were compared. For more than sixty years, it has remained the symbol of the era.

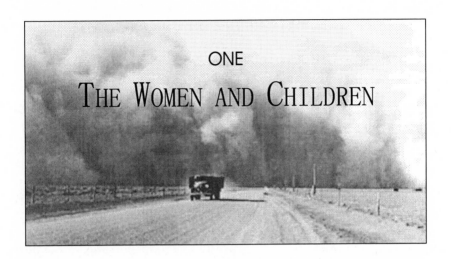

# ONE
# THE WOMEN AND CHILDREN

Women in the Dust Bowl years of the 1930s had the worst of it. Their daily routine consisted of an unending struggle to keep their houses free of dust, a job that was impossible to do because the wind blew almost constantly, and dust usually accompanied the wind. As you read their stories, you might wonder why they stayed in such a place. But you might also discover their strength and their steadying influence, as well as occasional humor they showed in the midst of the problems. Many of these women were children at the time of the storm, and their perspectives are different from those of their mothers and fathers in that they reflected the fear or lack of it, as their comments will show.

**Mrs. Sammy Cope, Liberal, Kansas:** [*From a letter.*] I was only six years old, but as this was the first Sunday after the burial of a baby brother, the family was at the cemetery just on the northwest side of Liberal—which is now in the city limits, but probably two miles from Main Street. At any rate, Father was visiting with the sexton and the family was generally "fooling around" that Sunday afternoon when a roar became apparent along with a visible black cloud of dirt coming from the northwest.

We were told to climb in the car and Father headed for town and to the Annex Cafe/Hotel owned by my grandfather, Roy Matkin, which was located just north of the railroad where the *Southwest Daily Times* newspaper is today. By the time we arrived in front of the cafe, the storm had hit and it was impossible to even see the lights in the cafe. Everyone was frightened and mother was crying, "Hang on to us, Rufus [King], the world is coming to an end!" Of course, it didn't, but it impressed me.

After what seemed like an endless time and Dad kept honking the horn, a knock on the (car) window came and a human link of men's arms from the car to the cafe carried each of us in out of the dusty environment. We spent the night in the hotel before going home to the farm eight miles south of town in the Oklahoma panhandle.

Many of our friends moved away and left their farms, but Dad held on, survived the holocaust of the West.

**Lyda Gilchriest, Pampa, Texas:** The kids were playing outside, and one of 'em ran in and told me [about this thing], and we looked out and this thing was like smoke r-o-l-l-i-n-g . . . was just rolling like that [*gestures hand over hand*] and it was dark when it enveloped the house. And there was actually dust behind the glass of pictures. But then houses were pretty much of a shell and [dust] just came through. I remember that year getting up in the morning, and I had a rug that had a pattern on it. You couldn't see the pattern. You could see your steps through the house. Those were the days.

**Frances Walls, Pampa, Texas:** I was across town [Miami, Texas] at my girlfriend's home, and everybody just started scuttling here and there and neighbors came and the clouds started rolling and they were hunting a cellar. And the thing that frightened me—I couldn't get across town to where Mother and Daddy were. . . . They just rolled!—the huge, huge clouds—and you turned a light on in the room and you couldn't see it. You put your hand up and you couldn't see it. And we started cramming into this cellar, and it was so full, and you really couldn't see whether the door was closed or not. But you knew it because you could taste sand in your mouth—very vividly—you could taste sand in your mouth. . . . [After the storm had abated] you were just more or less in a state of . . . just dazed. But even after the storm there was just silt all over everything—the ground, the

*Someone had a camera at the ready for these shots, taken seconds apart and showing clearly how awesome the cloud must have appeared to the person daring to hold the camera at the moment.*

—From the collection of F. L. Stallings, Sr.

sides of homes, tables—you could write your name—anything you wanted to. After you took a bath you really didn't feel clean. You were still covered with silt. Oily . . . it was sort of oily when you'd try to dust. You couldn't get it off. You couldn't sweep it out. . . . I really wanted to be with my Mother and Daddy if this was going to be the end of the world.

**Jean (Mrs. Harmon) Jenkins, Lubbock, Texas:** [*Interviewed in her home, where she was hanging a picture of a dust storm, painted by Texas Tech artist Clarence Kinkaid. A synopsis follows.*] She was in Floydada, Texas [northeast of Lubbock], that Sunday at a family gathering. She and her mother were in the kitchen when the storm came. She talked about the "intensity of the darkness and the pressure that seemed to affect everything, including the emotions." "The thickness of the darkness was overwhelming . . . it had a cloying effect, as if you were being touched by it." There were no storm windows or double windows, so the dust got in and on everything. The worst of it lasted only about fifteen minutes, then it lightened and just drifted.

The colors of the big storm were interesting, too, and visible in the rolling of the dust. She recalled a smattering of rain, too.

Afterward, they could not merely dust away the dust with a rag; cleaning required a damp cloth and a towel. Oiling the furniture was out of the question because it would simply make the dust harder to remove. In offices, the steel casement windows were totally unsatisfactory because the wind and dust would come in as though there were no window.

"When the earth moves, we're aware of it," she said at the end of the conversation.

**Helen Ruth Mackie, Pampa, Texas:** I was a senior in high school, and my father was the teacher out at Eli, and we lived in the teacherage. Used to be a parsonage for the preacher and teacherage for the teachers. . . . I can't remember what time of the day that it hit, other than in the afternoon. . . . We had been to Sunday school and church. . . . And all I can remember is grabbing sheets and blankets and towels and starting hanging [*sic*] them up on the [curtain rods?] because dirt just came in, you know, as it was rolling in. And the dry sheets didn't do a thing to keep it out, so we started pouring buckets of water. We had, I remember, a tub that we took baths in and washed mops and everything. And we filled it up with water and then we would dip the sheets in that tub of water and squeeze it out and then hang it up. We did that for hours . . . on the north windows especially . . . two sheets to a window. . . . We did that for hours while the dirt was coming in. This was well water from outside in the cistern.

Oh, and another thing. We didn't have a refrigerator, and Daddy had built this little frame out from one of the [kitchen] windows close to the stove, where Mother could just reach out, and we kept cloths all over the sides and the back of it, and one of my jobs was to keep water on it, you know, as much as I would remember. [During the storm] we didn't even think about that, and later we opened it up, and the butter didn't even look like butter—black, it was . . . had to throw that whole pound of butter away, of course.

**Erma Lee Barber, Pampa, Texas:** I was playing with the Rockwell twins across the street, and their father came down and told me I needed to go home because there was something terrible happening and then my daddy came after me. As soon as we got home, he tied wash rags with a string around our noses and mouths—and we had to stay in the house. He went outside and walked carefully to the neighbors' and put his hand on the houses and was walking around kind of surveying to see what was actually happening outside. When he came back in, he was . . . of course being a farmer and understanding wind and a little bit of soil blowing, he could not figure out exactly what was happening, so he said the best thing was to stay inside and wait it out.

Tents were made with sheets over our beds to keep the dust from settling down over us in the night. And then after that [in the morning] it was my job [*grimaces in disgust*] to wipe the table off ever' morning so Mother could set it. It would just have . . . just black with dirt. And shovel it out. On the way to school I loved to walk through the drifts of dust. I thought it was great. . . .

Doc Pursley and his wife went out on the front porch and

she says, "Oh, look out here, Doc, God's coming! It's the end of the world!" He went out and was looking around, and he says, "It looks more like hell to me!" . . . I wanted to stand there and watch it, but my daddy wouldn't let me.

**Maxine Hawkins, Pampa, Texas:** We went to an inside room and my dad turned the vacuum sweeper upside down in the room and I know we sat kind of in a circle and the vacuum sweeper was in the middle of the floor. And then we had the wet wash cloths over our faces, too, and I don't know how long the storm lasted, but evidently I went to sleep there because the next thing I knew it was morning and my mother came in to wake my sister and I, and she just put her arm down across us to wake us up and told us not to move. And then she just rolled the cover back. It was full of dirt. And then my sister and I sat up, and the pillow was white where our heads had been, and the rest of the pillow was black. And we had to get up the first thing and Mother had to shampoo our hair and give us a bath. . . . And then everything in the house was moved to the yard. . . . Everything went outside and the house was cleaned and brought back in. . . . I remember watching the next day about as much as I do the dirt storm for all the activity in the neighborhood and everybody's bedding was out on the line. . . .

[T]here was a boy that lived across the street from us that was a teenager. His name was Charles Patrick, and we thought that he was terribly wild, probably because he was about sixteen . . . . [W]hen the storm was coming, he had a gas mask I think left over from World War I, and he put on that gas mask and a heavy coat and had a whole bunch of rope and tied himself to the front porch. I never did know what happened to him.

**Mr. and Mrs. Lee Harrah, Pampa, Texas:** *Mr. Harrah:* Well, there was just a wall coming, just a-rolling, just a-tumbling and rolling, but once in a while there'd be dust devils, I guess you'd call them, carrying [dirt?] with it from the ground up. It wasn't like the dust devil that goes before a rain storm. It's a whirlwind but it . . . it's a kind of whirlwind, I guess. It went up in a column anyway. Just black and lighter gray columns with darkness and black behind.

*Mrs. Harrah:* And it was just rolling. You could just see it rolling.

**Mrs. Roger (Willie) McConnell, Pampa, Texas:** Well, it was on Sunday, and I was working with the young people at the church, and my oldest son, J.D., was an officer in there, so Glen Roger, my youngest, was too little to be left, and I went to take him to my sister's. And when I pulled in her drive, I saw it coming in. And you know, it was just terrible. Really, it was. It was just rolling on the ground . . . . Well, I ran back to the church as fast as I could—didn't let my little boy out—to pick J.D. up. Well, it hit us about two miles out. And I remember thinking that there's a little old place . . . out there going toward Borger, just a little ways out of town. I remember thinking though now, I had Glen Roger and J.D., in the car with me, "Now I may be going to die right now." I tell you it was the worst looking thing I ever saw. But we made it on home. I don't remember meeting any cars or anything, but we came on home.

[T]he next morning, oh, my house! I worked all morning—the kids was in school—worked all morning cleaning up the house and getting [the dust] out. And I belonged to the missionary society, too, and [it] met on Monday afternoon. I always tried to make that, too. But I didn't get my work done, and I decided, "Well, now God might punish me if I don't go to the missionary society. I'd better just leave this alone and go." And I did.

**Mrs. H. H. (Lois) Boynton, Pampa, Texas:** Hallie [her husband] was sick. He came home with strep throat, but they didn't call it that then. I saw that coming. It lay right in there, in the north, and the sun was bright and all, and I says, "Well, honey, that's not anything but plain old wind." He was kind of disturbed about it. I said, "That's not anything but wind." He said, "It's gonna be bad." And we heard a cow up there. We lived on Ram[?] Street then, and one of the men at the shop had gone to milk the cow. This happened. And he was out there just gettin' ready to come to the house, I guess. . . . And here came this man. He ended up at the lumberyard down there and then came on, found his way, came in and put that big can on the cupboard. It was pretty well filled, and it was just as black as coal, just as black as could be. It wasn't anything but black. Had to throw it out completely. But that's the way it happened. It was just like it is right now—beautiful. And when that hit, it was just like you went down into a cellar and closed the door. That's the way it was. You were completely blotted out. That's the way you felt.

Q: *Did you get the sheets hung up in time?*

No, that was later. We hung 'em all over the house. . . . We thought we were all going to die. Oh, we did. We just felt sure. . . . That was just terrible, terrible. And then the next morning you could still see the thing hanging . . . still heavy, but not like it was the night before. It had cleared out. But it was just heavy.

It was an experience you'll never, never forget. And we just thought sure we were all going to die. Or go someplace. Had to leave. And I left just as quick as school was out. I left and went to Arkansas, where my people lived. And took all those pictures to show 'em, and they just couldn't believe it.

**Mrs. Horace (Ruth) Brooks, White Deer, Texas:** This was on Sunday. The most beautiful Sunday. Oh, it was just perfect. I just read in that paper: temperature 90 degrees. The sun was shining, and we had two children—Kathryn, born in '28, and Jack, born in '32. After we had been to church and finished our dinner, my husband liked to hunt, so we got the children in the car, took his gun and we went out south of town and he was hunting and over there we saw this little ridge coming up. And we said, "Now what is that?" So he kept on hunting, and pretty soon it looked like it got about this [*gesture of about four feet*] high. And we kept on hunting and pretty soon we looked and it looked like we could touch a wall . . . now this is the way it looked, you know, like we could touch a wall, and over us was this coming over us, this wall here. . . . Then we realized what it was. Well, it was dust, and so there we were. And so Horace was so afraid that the children might choke to death, and it was so dark, but he says, "I think I remember where this windmill was, and I can go there and if there's some water there," which we knew there was, and he could wet his handkerchiefs and put it over the children's mouths to keep 'em from choking to death. So that's what we did. We stayed there, and it just got darker and darker and dustier and dustier, so finally he said, "I believe we can make it home." So we made it, we managed to get home, across the railroad track and to our house. And then when we got there, the neighbors were all so perturbed. You know what they thought? They thought it was the end of the world.

**Mrs. H.L. (Ruby) Burke, Beaver, Oklahoma:** We'd been living [in Beaver] during the dust storms, and we thought we'd seen everything in dust storms during those years, but this was the unusual thing. I know it was a pretty Sunday afternoon, for those Dust Bowl times, so my husband, Herbert, and our son, Leo, and a friend, Jean Reimuth, and I, we decided to go out riding, and we went toward Booker way. We left our daughter, Theda May, with the Green family, which is a wonderful family close by. She didn't care to go. And so coming home about 4:00 P.M., that's when we saw this thing come up in the north, and so I . . . I don't think my husband was as frightened as I was, but I said, "Let's stop at the next farm house because . . . oh, something's behind that." And he says, "Oh, maybe we can get on home." Well, we stopped at the farm house. We just barely got in, and the lady had a bucket of water right inside her door. It wasn't a modern home, and she had this wash stand, basin and all, and she gave us some towels. We didn't know her. And she says, "Wet these towels, and we'll go to the . . . what she called a cave because it was a cave that you go into from the house. We used to have those outside, you know, and you'd have to go outside to a cave for shelter from storms. And then she lighted a lamp down in there. We could hardly see that little burner in the lamp. Oh, it was pitch dark—inky dark. We just never did see anything like it. But later it kind of blew over in thirty or forty minutes, and we came out and everything she had in the house was covered with dust. You couldn't see what anything looked like. The prints or anything. She had polished floors when we went in, and throw rugs—well, had braided and crocheted rugs, and they were just mounds. Looked like mounds of dust. Oh, it was terrible.

Well, we finally started home when we thought we could see a little bit. And then at times it would get darker and then get lighter. It was kind of a reddish sand storm. I don't know why . . . where this dirt . . . our dirt's kind of reddish, too, at times, you know, this top soil. Sometimes we get it from Texas and Oklahoma and it goes north, and then we get the northern soil and it comes back. You know how it does. So my husband got out once, and we couldn't tell for sure if we were in the road because we couldn't see the cap of the radiator. And then after he got out of the car, trying to feel where the fence was to see where we were, then we were frightened because we didn't know whether he could get back to the car or not. He should have had a rope leash to go out there so he could follow it back, but of course this was all unexpected.

As I said, this was a beautiful Sunday afternoon until this came up. Well, during the meantime, we had a church meeting for the elders at the church, and they became so frightened, one of my friends told me, she said, "Those that could . . . could see to get to the altar, they prayed, and those sat in the pews." And said, "There was one or two that would just lie down in the aisle because they thought this was the end of the world." They thought, "Well, now, the Bible tells us that the Lord will come back in a cloud." But they thought a cloud from the sky, naturally, and said, "Maybe they meant this was the cloud." And they thought that was a queer way for Him to appear—in a cloud of dust. Well, you know, they've predicted the end of the world ever since time, but it didn't come.

Well, Herb, my husband, was postmaster at that time, and also during that time people ordered baby chickens, and they came to the post office. Well, we couldn't call these people, and so we took the chickens home and set 'em on the back porch. And, evidently when we left, we didn't get the door closed properly—I don't think it could have blown open because we had a new home—but anyway, when we came home, the door was open and the chickens were covered with dust, and we just knew they'd be smothered to death. But they hadn't. We only lost two. I dusted 'em off, and got 'em some water, and they survived. But we did call the people. The lines still worked. And they came and got 'em that evening. It lit up enough that evening so we could see to get around a little bit.

Oh, but my house, you should have seen it! It was just terrible!

**Betty Fisher Williams (Mrs. Paul), Liberal, Kansas:** We were in a church service and people kept getting up and going out, and they'd come back in. And somebody else would go out and come back in. And then church just broke up. We just run out to watch and then of course we all run back in the church and I can remember my mother gathering us all around. . . . I was from Stevens County, twelve miles west of here, so we were at a little country church that afternoon. It was the middle of the afternoon . . . Sunday afternoon . . . broke up the wedding. You reckon those people ever finished their vows? They may be running around today not married. . . . Pretty soon [during the church service] you could see the dirt rolling, and then pretty soon you knew it wasn't rain. It was going to be another one of them dirty dusters. . . . Well, it was different dirt. It wasn't even our dirt. We never could figure whose dirt it was. It's not our dirt. [*Another voice on the tape:* "It was Dakota dirt."] Well, except when it would come out of the south. Then we would blame Texas. It was dark all the rest of the day. It stayed dark, and the wind blew and blew and blew and blew . . . you didn't know what to do, what to think. . . . There was no one but what figured this was the end of the world. What do you do to get ready for the end of the world?

You knew something was happening, but you couldn't hear nothing. There was no commotion. You knew something was happening because people would run out. You knew it wasn't just your rainstorm—you'd be hearing thunder and lightning. You knew something was going on out there. Whoever was on the stage, they'd start up then they'd stop and then they'd start up. Somebody's come in and *"psssht, psssht, psssht"* and up they'd go and out. Everybody wanted to roll up their car windows, and so finally they just quit.

We stayed there. Nobody moved. You couldn't see your hand in front of your face. It was absolutely pitch dark. Nobody moved. . . . I sort of remember finding our way home because the car lights wouldn't penetrate it. We just didn't dare move. We stayed there for, I expect, two hours. . . nobody said anything.

[Afterward] we would have gatherings. The women would laugh or kindy [*sic*] challenge, "Well, now, how many buckets of dirt did you get out of that one?" We finally began to measure buckets, each jokingly trying to outdo the other by announcing

*Mrs. Robert Lott, a young mother with a tiny child, had good reason to leave her apartment and seek better shelter in her in-laws' home when she saw what loomed minutes away.*

—Courtesy of *Southwest Daily News*, Liberal, Kansas

it in bucketfuls. Then it got to be, "We had more dirt than you had, *ha, ha, ha.*"

**Mrs. Clifford (Maxine) Browne, Liberal, Kansas:** I was teaching in a school up clear in the extreme northern part of [Seward] county. And I was home for the weekend, and my husband, Cliff, and I were doing the dishes. He was drying the dishes for me, and we were going to go somewhere that afternoon, and we went outside to carry out some things to throw away. And he looked up north—we were living on an old ranch down on the Cimarron River—and he looked up north toward the old Pyle Ranch, and he called to me and says, "Come out here!" And I looked, and it was just a huge blackness in the north. And we stood there and watched, and as it got closer, you couldn't see a thing beyond it. It was just coming in. And whereas most of them seemed to be rolling, this one just seemed to be kind of slipping along. Not so much rolling, just coming. And when it got fairly close, Cliff went in—we didn't have electricity, of course—and he lighted the gasoline lamps. And when it hit, it was an eerie darkness—not like the darkness of night, but terrible. And we were in a room that was about 14 x 15—we could see each other with that bright gasoline lamp—we could see each other, but it was just like looking through a veil.

**Mrs. Robert Lott (Irene) Kennedy, Liberal, Kansas:** I didn't know this Mr. Wilson whose funeral it was. I think it was Mr. Wilson. And they had his funeral at the Methodist Church. And I was just a young married woman with a tiny baby . . . . It was a beautiful Sunday, just gorgeous, and of course we lived in this apartment. It was a very nice, new apartment. The Haddix apartments were brand new then, and that's where we lived. And somehow or other I looked out or my husband looked out, and we saw this terrible thing coming, and we decided we'd better take that tiny baby and go over to his parents'. So we did, and we went over there. And just as we ran in, it hit. And I turned on the front porch light, and you couldn't see one thing of that porch light—not a particle. And my sister-in-law was at the funeral. She was . . . our biggest concern. Now, I know afterwards a lot of people said they felt the world was coming to an end.

Never entered my mind. I didn't have stuff like that on my mind. And so, anyhow, we were concerned about my sister-in-law, and lo and behold, in all this darkness—this blackness—she came crawling in. She crawled from that Methodist Church.

*Q: How far was that from the church?*

It'd be just two, a little over two [blocks]. Two blocks, all right. And she probably knew she could. She should never have done it. She had to cross two streets, and if cars had been coming, why, she wouldn't have known it, and they wouldn't either, because no light penetrated that darkness. And so here she comes. She had crawled all the way from that church to the house over there. I never saw anything like it—I'm not joking. I had come to Liberal from eastern Kansas, and we never had anything like that there.

*Maxine Browne:* We hadn't either, honey, 'til then.

**Bob and Mildred Hill, Turpin, Oklahoma:** [*Because the Hills were in the same place at the same time during the storm, their comments are together. Their perceptions do differ somewhat, though.*] *Mildred:* I've lived in Beaver County all my life. But I happened to be at my mother's in Liberal, Kansas, and . . . I was sitting out in the car with my boyfriend when all at once this thing rolled in. And you couldn't even see your finger this close [*four inches*] to you. It was coming in the car, and well, it lasted all night and the biggest part of the day the next day. And then for days all this dust settled. . . .

We just sat there in the car. And then finally I went in to my mother's and I stayed. And I don't remember what he done, whether he tried to make it home or. . . . He had a sister that lived in Liberal. Might have made it to her place. I just can't remember . . . back that far. But I know it was bad and it was scary.

[It was a] real pretty day that day, and like I said, that just started rolling in. You could see it coming, you know. And it just rolled . . . . It *really* rolled. You can almost see it roll there [*holding up a photograph*], and that's the way it came in.

*Bob:* And the dirt storm, now that was April the 14th of '35 is when the big one come up, and Mildred might have told you. Mildred and I was sitting in a car up at Liberal in front of her mother's house, and her stepdad come out of the house, oh, it

*These two photos demonstrate how the storm looked to those seeing it approach, especially as remembered by Bob Hill (next page): "It was just like a slow moving big cloud of smoke and black dirt and just moved real slow. It would just cover a house up gradually. You could see it move from the north end of a house to the south end . . . it seemed like it took quite a period of time. It probably was just a few seconds."*

must've been maybe a hour or two before that thing hit. He said, "We're gonna get a bad dirt storm." He said he could see it just above the horizon over in the north. And I couldn't see it, so I guess we was just kids. I would have been nineteen, see, and she was a little older than I am. She was probably about twenty, probably going on twenty-one or something like that. And we sat there in that car, you know, and just talking, I guess, like a couple of kids would. . . . And after while her stepdad come out again and, well, this thing had come up quite a ways. And then after while, we seen what it was going to be, you know. It was a terrible black cloud. As that thing drifted over the houses, it was just like . . . well, I can't explain it. . . . It was just like a slow moving big cloud of smoke and black dirt and it just moved real slow. It would just cover a house up gradually. You could see it move from the north end of a house to the south end . . . it seemed like it took quite a period of time. It probably was just a few seconds, but it seemed like it was a minute or two from the time you couldn't see the north side of the house . . . before you couldn't see the south end. And it was just as clear as day up 'til that hit. It was just as sunshiny as any sunshiny day you could see, and after that hit I just felt like I was suffocated. . . . I just run out of air, oxygen. And as far as I know, they turned the lights on in the house, but we couldn't see the house. I turned my car lights on, and the beam of light maybe out there looked like it was shining out about three feet.

**Mrs. W. H. (Donna Belle) Schultz, Liberal, Kansas:** [*I asked Mrs. Schultz whose funeral was being held that day.*] Wilson. Lee Wilson. He wasn't buried until the next day. I had just come out [of the church], and they were viewing the body [inside the church] at the Methodist Church, and I looked up and here were these black clouds moving toward town. Well, I knew what they were. . . . So I thought, "Well, they hadn't turned the lights on." And the pallbearers were out there, you know, stationed. . . . My car was parked a block away, and so I thought, "Well, I'd better get away from this church before it gets dark and I can't see across the street." So I went directly to my car, and the thing that surprised me was that the minute I put my hand on the door knob, why here . . . birds preceded this black dust storm. A

*One of hundreds of photos that clearly show the size of the rolling mass of dirt as it approaches a western Kansas town.*

—Courtesy of Kansas State Historical Society

bunch of birds flew by, and then all of a sudden it turned so black I couldn't see my hands in front of my face. The dust just came in that car like the doors weren't closed. So I sat there for—it seemed like hours—until it got light enough that, you know, the darkness left. But you still couldn't see anything. But everybody turned their lights on. So I counted the blocks. I started home, and I was by myself. So I counted the blocks from the church. And quite a while later a friend that was there called to see if I'd got home all right. And no one was home but the cat, and the cat was . . . it was a two-story brick house and the cat had climbed up the brick wall to the kitchen window—it was a yellow angora cat. It was so dusty you couldn't tell what color it was. I took the cat off the screen and took it in the house. If you left a window up, you couldn't tell whether you had a rug on the floor or whether there wasn't any.

I had a brother-in-law that lived at Dalhart, and he worked for the Rock Island [Railroad], and of course seen on the telegraph—they got that—and at his boardinghouse he kept telling them it was moving this way, and of course he expected it because he knew it was moving so many miles an hour and they didn't pay any attention to him until it hit. . . . It started up in the Dakotas and Nebraska and just kept moving southward.

**Maidee Thompson, Hall County, Texas:** [*Recorded by Helen Ruth Mackie. A synopsis by Mackie follows.*] At this time she was teaching in Hall County, six miles northeast of Turkey, Texas. She lived in a teacherage just like I did, only hers was just a little lean-to; the principal and his wife lived in the original two rooms of the old school building. So she said be sure and tell you how much of a mansion she lived in. It was made out of beaver-board and the roof was tin, so when the wind and the rain and the dirt and the sand and the rocks came, she got 'em just almost as if she'd been sitting outside, 'cause, she said, beaverboard doesn't keep out very much. . . .

On this particular day, around five o'clock or a little after, she had heard on a little battery-power radio that this big black sand storm had hit Amarillo, and they were warning people as far south as could hear 'em that this was coming and it was as black as night. . . . She said that when she heard that, she went outside and looked all to the north and said that it did look rather strange, but she couldn't tell too much other than as if the dirt was blowing on Red River. See, Buffalo Flat—how far from that river? 'bout six, seven, ten miles? Ten. And she said when the wind blew, it kicked up the dirt, er, sand, easily, but the radio had said this was a black duster and the dirt out of Red River naturally was red so she knew this was something else coming. . . . She went out and told the people [going to the school house for church service] what she had just heard on the radio. And they never did let their kids or wives out of the wagons. They just drove 'em up into the school yard and turned around, and ever' one of 'em headed home just as fast as they could. So after all of them left, then, she said, "I wonder why somebody didn't ask me to go home with them?" She was there alone, so she went to the school house 'cause it was built out of some rocks and cement. It was definitely better than the teacherage was. Anyway, she went to the school house and stayed "at least a couple of hours because it did get so dark." And she lighted the gasoline lantern that was up there and said then she did not remember any wind at all ahead of it. Then when it hit, she said it was terrific. . . . I said, "Well, did you remember anything that any of 'em said the next day?" And she said, "Well, they were all trying to figure out where it had come from and why it acted so strange and different to the other wind that had come and dirt and so forth."

**Mrs. Eunice Bohot, Pampa, Texas:** I think I was preparing something in the kitchen about that time. It was about five o'clock, wasn't it? And all at once it came, you know, sudden. Everything just turned dark. And then I finally wondered where the children were. And they were out on the vacant lot . . . one of them, especially Patsy, and we finally got her inside. And everybody was just flabbergasted because it was dark as pitch. We had to turn the lights on in the house. And somebody said, "Well, what has happened?" And we just didn't know because the wind was blowing so hard with it, and dark, too. But we all got in the house, then we wondered about my husband, where he was, 'cause he worked out in the [oil] field a lot. And we didn't know where to find him. And this was going on, I don't know how long.

And somebody said, "Turn on the sweeper." So we turned on the sweeper, thinking that it—the dust—had gotten into the house, too, you know, I mean the dark . . . some of the dust had come in before we could close the doors. And then somebody said, "Well, turn on the air conditioner." We had one of those window evaporative coolers, you know, and they said turn on those and maybe that would get the dust so we could breathe better. Seems like it got in the house to some extent. Then we didn't know how to get it out after it got in there. Then finally we all got settled down. And I don't know how long this was going on before somebody called and said that Miami had sent us a warning that this was on its way, but we didn't get the call before it hit. Word came from Miami that it was coming, that there was to be . . . everybody be prepared that there was a dark cloud coming. They didn't know what it was, you know, at first, just thought it was a dark cloud. But the dust and sand and dirt with it. We didn't know what to expect.

Seems like I had to do a lot of scraping and running the sweeper and cleaning out windows and places that we had collected a lot more dust. And I had nearly always had help, had a girl to help me. And it seems like that we had . . . seems like we had to either sweep a lot of the walls down with a . . . we took a broom and our towel and wiped out a lot of the dust that had collected.

[*The evaporative cooler Mrs. Bohot referred to is still widely used in dry climates, but its effectiveness in a dust storm would certainly be questionable since outside air is drawn into the house through excelsior wetted by dripping water through it. Any dust at all would probably clog up the filter, though the air would be cooled and dampened as long as it could penetrate the filter.*]

**Per (Mrs. Martin) Stubbe, south of Shamrock, Texas:** I was just thirteen years old at the time, and it was very frightening to see this cloud . . . well, we thought it was a cloud. We didn't know it was just a dust storm. And we always went to the cellar regardless, because my mother had been shocked by lightning, at one time, and she could feel the electricity in the air any time a cloud was coming up day or night, and it would wake her up if it were at night. So we always went to the cellar, and when we saw this big black cloud rolling in from the north, which was very unusual for anything to come from the north. Most of our clouds came from the south or southwest. So we looked, but it was still, the air was real still and calm. The atmosphere was not the typical atmosphere that you have when a real cloud comes up. And no wind in front of it. . . . and this was very unusual because during that time, you know, the wind blew, blew, blew, blew, blew dirt. But our dirt was a different color from this black dirt that came in. But anyway, we always took a change of clothes to the cellar, and we grabbed our extra change and went to the cellar. And then of course as it began to roll in and settle, we realized that it was, you know, just dirt. . . . I wouldn't say it was a storm because it didn't blow like that; it just came in—it rolled, kind of rolled in and settled. That's what it did.

**Jennie Rose Benton:** [*From Panhandle-Plains Historical Museum files.*] The cloud that arose in the north on that beautiful Sunday afternoon was in its immensity both beautiful and terrifying. It was not the usual brown dust cloud, but a thing of many shadows approaching silently, but relentlessly on toward its helpless victims. Then it hit. It was, indeed, an awesome feeling to sit in a room full of people and not be able to see those sitting across the room. There was nothing to do but wait and wonder the effect of all this on our future and on our health.

**Myrtle Davidson, Pampa, Texas:** [*Copied from the diary of Myrtle Davidson, grandmother of Fred Vanderberg, Sr.*] Sunday, April 14 [1935] A beautiful day until 7 o'clock this Eve, and one of those things come up from the north east. My it looked viscious [*sic*] all black with white streaks and rolling and twisting coming right on us, but it was only a bad dust storm probaly [*sic*] had some carbon black & smoke from the oil fields. Myrtle [Simmons] and Mr. Gilmore had supper with us. We came very near not seeing it before it hit as it was black as night for a few minutes [then] it cleared up.

**Juanita Pond, Pampa, Texas:** [*Phone interview.*] The family rushed down to the cellar, thinking it might be a tornado, but after the storm hit, the dust was so heavy in the cellar as to make breathing impossible. So they had to rush back to the house, where they covered the windows with sheets and blankets, which kept out some but not much of the dirt. A neighbor boy in the house watching the dust said, on looking out and being unable to see anything, "Well, it got Grandma; guess it'll get us next."

**Phoebe Osborne Reynolds, Pampa, Texas:** [*Phone interview. A synopsis follows.*] The family was traveling from Plainview to Miami and was in the vicinity of Canyon in midafternoon when the storm hit. The most memorable parts of the storm were her mother's absolute calm and serenity. Also, she remembers thinking at the time that the storm must be a little like being buried in a sandpile.

**Maggie Gill (Mrs. Elmo), Miami, Texas:** [*Synopsis of interview at Roberts County Museum.*] She lived three and a half miles south toward Laketon. The storm came in "rolling off the hills." It looked like a tornado so they rushed to the cellar, but her husband looked out and said, "It's nothing but dirt." But it was "the blackest one." They had a daughter who was five months old, and Mrs. Gill "figured it would choke her to death." They hung wet sheets over the windows. A cousin of hers, coming to town on the day of the storm, thought it was the end of the world. After the storm she "took a broom and swept and scooped" dirt out of the house. It was piled up outside all over everything. "Oh, mercy!"

**Mrs. Bonnie Williamson, Miami, Texas:** [*Synopsis of interview in her home.*] At the time of the storm she had four children, one a baby boy about a month old. Her husband was in the CCC [Civilian Conservation Corps] and was out in the country. They lived in an old house, and on this beautiful day the sun was shining and she cleaned house all morning. There had been several days of dust during the preceding week and the house was "covered with dirt." After dinner she went over to a neighbor's house about two miles away, leaving the house open. The children were all outside playing, but one came running into the house yelling, "Somethin' comin'! Rollin'!" It was between 4:30 and 5:00. The dirt rolled in—black—but while driving back toward home, the car died [probably from static electricity]. Once it got started again, the lights didn't do any good, so they "moseyed on home"—about a mile and a half. "When we got home, there was a light on, and when we went in there was a boy in the house who had got to the house. He went in and closed the windows, but it was too late; the house was filled"— worse than it was before she had cleaned that morning. The kids were all scared to death— "just a-bawlin' "—and Mrs. Williamson "thought the world was coming to an end." There was hardly any wind. The house had no running water, no plumbing, and no electricity.

**Mrs. Jack (Willie) McClary, Dumas, Texas:** [*A synopsis follows.*] She was living on a farm northeast of Dumas. She had four children, "just tots," and was away from the house polishing their new car. The children were playing and one came up screaming about a storm coming. She told the biggest child to "grab Ned before it hits!" They were rushing toward the house, but the storm hit just before they got into the house. They had reached the screened porch that led to the kitchen. In the kitchen it was already pitch dark and she stumbled over children in the floor. She lighted the kerosene lantern and put it into the window, hoping her husband could see it, but when her husband did see it, he thought it was car lights coming from the other direction and so he wandered out into a field. He kept yelling, however, and finally was heard and got into the house. She was afraid her youngest child might choke to death in the dust, so she draped a wet sheet over the crib.

**Elva Jean Shepic, Canyon, Texas:** I don't remember much about the storm except that we went into the nearest place, and the nearest place was the Black Lantern, a saloon. Mother was not at all pleased that this was the kind of place we found. Being caught in Amarillo was bad enough, but in a saloon!

**Eleanor (Mrs. Andrew) McNamara, Pampa, Texas:** [*From a letter.*] Memories of Palm Sunday, April 14, 1935, a beautiful day in Pampa, Texas.

My husband, Andrew McNamara, and I lived on the Texas Company Bowers lease, in the breaks [places where the prairie ends and erosion has caused ditches or even canyons to be formed] close to the branch of the Red River; 1-1/2 miles from Bowers City; 10 miles south of Pampa. The lease house had three rooms and 1/2 of a bath. Andrew was production forman [*sic*].

We had gone into Pampa, Saturday, to buy groceries, spend the nite with my parents (Mr. and Mrs. A.B. Zahn) and attend mass in Holy Souls Church Sunday. After dinner April 14, Andrew took our two daughters, Eleanor Ann 5-1/2 yrs and Catherine 3-1/2 with him to check on oil wells south of the Bowers line.

I soon left for home with my son Bernard who was 18 mos. I was 7-1/2 mos pregnant. I arrived home, put Bernard in the baby bed, while I unloaded the car. I went out again to put the car in the garage, which was 150 feet away, when I saw this mountain of a black cloud which stretched across the horizon. It did not seem to have wind in it, by the time I ran back to the house it hit. Day into nite. I wet a sheet to cover the baby, pulled the shades down, turned on the lights and prayed for the safety of my husband and two small daughters.

When Andrew left the oil lease, he saw the black cloud, he tried to make it home, but when he couldn't see the road, he stopped at a house for shelter, could hardly find the door. They got home three hours later, covered with fine dust and wet rags over their noses and nouths. We agreed it was a terrible experience.

The Texas Co. left their men off Monday, so they could help clear their homes, furniture was taken outside, curtains and shades removed, dirt was hanging on the walls, everything was covered with it. It took days to get back to normal living.

**Mrs. J.F. (Hazel) Clark, Pampa, Texas:** [*From a letter.*] We'll never forget it, living in an oil field shack in the middle of Mr. W. W. Harrah's pasture. When we saw that thing coming it looked like a rolling and boiling oil field fire but we knew it wasn't as it covered all the north direction. Inside our house was a thick fog of dust. We used wet wash rags etc. to our faces. And after the dust storm we had to clean house. I mean take curtains pictures etc. down. I feel we got more out in the country than those in town. We were lucky to be at home and not caught out on black Sunday as many others. It was a beautiful Sunday.

**Alma (Mrs. Charles) Seitz, Miami, Texas:** [*From a letter.*] [T]he duster that is remembered above all others is the one that actually rolled in 14 April 1935 and many people thought the world was coming to an end. That duster crept in, not with a terrific wind but rolled as if it were smoke and it completely obliterated the view of everything behind it. Charlie and Coony Lawrence [Charlie Seitz and B. A. Lawrence], who worked for us at that time, were out in the pasture horseback. They said it changed from light to dark so quickly that the horses just jumped along instead of going at a natural gait. We lived at the old Jim Johnston place. I just happened to be looking out at the door and saw the screen of darkness as it moved over the cemetery, and after watching it for a minute, decided that I had better pull the window blinds to keep out the dirt and dust that we had become used to, and before I reached the last window, the darkness was so bad that it was difficult to tell the windows from the walls. Everything was completely dark. It was midnight dark. Dust particles were so dense the coal oil lamp was barely visible. It was just a little yellow flicker. It threw no light out around it. Neither did electric lights, so I have been told. People did go to cellars, for they knew nothing better to do. After an hour or so Charlie and Coony did get to the house. The story has always been that a wise thing to do if lost is to give the horse the reins, and he will take the person home, but that was not the case in that instance. The horses were lost; they could not tell which way to go or what to do. They just jumped along as if they were going over a cliff into a bottomless pit. Wendell was not a year old, and I remember carrying him and holding Charles Arthur by the hand and just waiting to see what the outcome was going to be.

[*This letter is part of page 230 from* Tottys and Totty Ties, *a family history. The ranch mentioned was about a mile and a half southwest of Old Mobeetie in Wheeler County, Texas.*]

**Avanelle Milligan Stone, Waco, Texas:** [*From a letter.*] I was seventeen and would graduate from White Deer High School the next month and lived on an oil lease about 5 miles north of Skellytown, Texas. It was a Sunday and with my usual Sunday afternoon date we had started into Skellytown for sodas at the local drug store with friends. As we left my home, we noticed the

Panhandle Dust-Storm
April 14, 1935

The Sunday drive to get sodas at a drug store for a young couple was interrupted when they watched the dust erase from sight one oil derrick after another on its way to the car they were in. Her white linen blouse never was white after that, Mrs. Stone said. The derricks in the photo were not the ones she refers to; these were in a different lease.

—Smith Studio Photo

bank of dust in the north and my father was a bit hesitant about my leaving but we did. We were between my home and Skellytown when it reached us. It rolled in from the sky down and as it reached oil drilling rigs which were lighted from the crown to the drilling floor as it was nearing dusk, they were immediately blotted out or blacked out from sight. Birds flew around in front of the wall of dust excitedly as if seeking refuge from a storm. When the storm reached us we turned on car lights but they did not penetrate so we pulled to the side of the road and stopped to wait it out.

We had not been stopped long when we could see, though dimly, car lights coming toward us. It stopped across the road from us and went out. Soon a man came across the road and asked if he could bring his wife and children into the car with us because one of the windows in his car was broken out. So they all came into the car with us and we sat out the dust storm together. After it cleared where one could see enough to drive, they thanked us very kindly and went on their way. By this time night had fallen. We drove on into Skellytown and had our sodas.

Meanwhile, back at my home were my father, mother and two brothers. My parents wet bedsheets and hung them over windows and doors to catch the fine incoming dust, fine as powder. Actually, it seemed I was better off than the family although the house was well enough built for those times. My mother told me later, "You will never know how worried your father was about you that night."

I was wearing a white linen blouse and I can promise you that after the dust storm that blouse was gray. The dust in our area had a lot of dark or black soil in it.

. . . P.S. An afterthought—In the Texas Panhandle area, this is referred to as "The Big Black Duster of '35." As to the effects, I certainly had no thoughts that it was the end of the world, neither did any of my family—it was just another dust storm, only more severe and blacker than any at that time or since.

**Bula Flynn, Pampa, Texas:** [*From a letter.*] I would like to say I was 18 at the time of the blackest and worst dust storm of the time. I was living in Amarillo. My father tore up rags and stuffed

in cracks around the windows and doors. Papa also wet cloths
and we held them on our faces so we could breath [*sic*] better.
Back in the 30's we had to hang out the washing & sometime we
would just get 'em hung up & here would come a dust storm, we
had to take 'em down & put 'em in the tub. We set the table with
the plates upside down & kept a cloth over the table. I remember I would sprinkle the floor with water before I could sweep
then mop. It sure was disgusting to keep house. You couldn't tell
when the wind and dirt would stop. There would be days & days
the sky was red or black from so much in the sky.

[*She writes in her letter: "I work at a nursing home here in
Pampa, and I was talking to some of the old timers, and here are some
remarks they made."*]

**Thelma Paris of Miami, Texas:** We were up at Jamie Talley's
house in Miami, Texas, and Paul Paris was with us. He said,
"Look out! there sure is comming [*sic*] up a terrible cloud. We run
got in our 1935 Ford & rushed home. We run in the house & I
had flour & food out so we covered up the food & went to the
storm celler [*sic*]. Pa said, "I'll strike a match so you can see to get
down the steps—you couldn't see the match. The dirt was thick.
I never have seen anything like it. The dirt was more like ashes.

**Fanny Bailley of Miami, Texas:** I saw a black cloud comming
[*sic*], I didn't know if it was a fire or what it was. It was pitch dark.
I had a cake in the oven half done, I turned out the burners and
went to the dug-out celler [*sic*]. We had to take a tub up stairs to
put the dirt in.

**Blanch Jenkins, Pampa, Texas:** I was making bread and that
biscuit dough was anything but white.

**Anna Reed, Great Falls, Virginia:** [*In Pampa at the time of the
storm. The following is from a letter.*] The only thing that I have
never understood is this: I remember standing on the front
porch of our house (it was on Crest Street) and looking toward
the east to see the storm rolling in. I thought these storms blew
in from the west. It looked like a horizontal tornado—black and
boiling and hugging the horizon. I remember there was a little

girl visiting me and she was all upset to the point of being hysterical. Later I remember that Mr. George Saunders said for her not to worry that it was not the end of the world or words to that effect . . . it was only a dust storm. Of course, since he was a rancher I'm sure he knew it was more important than we knew, but he knew we were too young to understand the far reaching effects of the storm. I have always thought that the storm "happened" on Easter Sunday. George Saunders was the uncle of Horace [a school friend].

I remember that I wanted to argue with my elders who said you could not see the wind. I could see the wind . . . at least the dust in the wind, but I was convinced that I could see it . . . .

**Hortense (Mrs. William) Wilder, Akron, Ohio:** [*In Lubbock, Texas, at the time of the storm. From a letter.*] I . . . remember that after a bit of complete blackness it lightened up and was a reddish sandstorm—from black to red. Where did the red come from and how was it picked up? I don't remember reading any facts on that strange storm. But, oh, that rolling black cloud on the ground swallowing up everything in its path!

**Sylvia Wesendonk, Lubbock, Texas:** [*From a letter.*] The black duster of April 1935 was a once-in-a-lifetime experience for those of us who were in Lubbock, Texas, that afternoon. And now, 47 years later, I'm trying to picture it as I remember it.

On Sunday afternoon, I was at my parents' home on a small farm south of Lubbock, which in 1983 [*date of the letter*] would be in the vicinity of Indiana Avenue and 70th Street. We, my parents, and brother and I, were playing cards when the room suddenly became dark. Our first reaction was to step outside the east door onto the porch to see what was happening.

There was nothing to see as it was dark, a blackish-brown darkness: we were immediately aware of dust. It was still—no wind and no breeze. It was not a sandstorm! This was different! Within minutes, or perhaps seconds, it was becoming lighter as though a cloud had lifted, or passed over, though a very fine and powdery dust was settling everywhere. We realized the cloud was moving to the south. In this stillness there was an eerie feeling. With a lot of concern we were questioning the cause, the source, and the answer for this phenomenon. The dust was from afar as it was not the color nor the texture of Lubbock's soil, for it was darker and finer. This dust continued to settle for several hours.

Mother and father (Mr. and Mrs. Andy Wilson) had been in Lubbock since early 1890 and had never seen anything like this storm. We were not really frightened, for it was over so quickly. There had been many stories of the dust storms in the Dust Bowl area that we accepted this strange and unusual occurrence as another part of the Dust Bowl storms.

**Mrs. A. B. Davis, Lubbock, Texas:** [*Synopsis of an untaped interview.*] On 14 April 1935 her husband was out north of town (near the current coliseum site) in a polo match. It was moderately windy and somewhat cloudy. Cars, as usual on that field, were parked around the field and the observers sat on the cars to watch the match. Then in rolled the dust and turned it dark as night. Everyone was told to turn on car lights, but the car lights could not penetrate the darkness. The absolute blackness lasted a short time, then came a slight shower, of mud.

Back home, we learned that the black servant had been frightened almost to death. He thought it was the end of the world.

**Mrs. Ruth L. Lowray, McLean, Texas:** [*From a letter.*] I remember the day. Some friends had us to lunch. Baked a birthday cake with one candle on it for our daughter (Juanita Hargis), and I drove to take a friend home. As we were returning, the storm hit us downtown Pampa. We had to stop the car because of the black dust storm. Was holding our daughter on my lap, could not see her or the car lights. I put a blanket over her head and held her tightly. It was so frighting [*sic*], don't know how long it lasted.

My husband was a gauger for Texaco Inc. at the time. Said he had to put a wet cloth over his face to gauge the oil tanks when it passed over because of the dust. A day we'll never forget.

**Mrs. Henrimae Christopher, Amarillo, Texas:** [*Panhandle-Plains Historical Museum files.*] The first black dust storm that I remember was on a Sunday afternoon in April 1935. It could be seen as far as Stinnett, rolling in from Colorado. It was frightening but beautiful. As it rolled along, the wind picked up different colored soils. As we saw it approaching, it had all the colors of the rainbow.

Some people from Borger were visiting friends of ours that Sunday. When they noticed the big cloud to the north, they decided to leave for home. They had gotten only two blocks away when the dust storm struck. They could not see how to drive; their lights did not penetrate the dust; it was totally dark. They got out of their car and crawled along the curb back to the house which they had just left. They had to spend the night and go home the next day.

The first black duster was very frightening. People did not know what was happening. Some thought the enemy had suddenly struck with a bomb. I had a friend living at the Palo Duro Apartments. He said he and the other men tried to remain calm, but that women were crying from fright; some were praying.

This first one was just the beginning of many—some as bad and some not quite so black. They were all most unpleasant.

**Ethel Johnson, Pampa, Texas:** We were living at 615 North Nelson at the time that this duster hit. . . . I was just a kid, of course. But we had some friends who lived down the block named Hodge, and I had been down to their house and some of the girls and I were standing out in the street, which was unpaved, just talking, and we happened to turn around and look toward the north and here was this tremendous wall of black. We had no idea what it was. So we watched it for a few minutes, and it got closer and bigger, and we decided we had better go to our respective homes. So we parted company and I went to my house and she to hers. And I turned around and looked back just before I went in the door and it had become much closer and much larger and almost filled the sky, and you could see the dirt rolling like a carpet unrolling, only it was an awful mixed up carpet because it was different shades of black and gray and brown. I got on in the house and my father (Dr. H. L. Wilder) and my brother-in-law (Loyd Stallings) and my brother (Henry Wilder) decided they would go outside and stand at the corner of the house until whatever this thing was that was coming hit. Of course by that time we had decided it was dirt. So they did, and it almost . . . the wind was so strong it almost knocked them over, but didn't last very long fortunately, but the house filled with dirt, dust, all over. It was black. It was dark. We had to turn on lights. They came back into the house and they were completely covered from head to foot with dirt. Ears, eyes, nostrils, if they'd had a mustache, it would have been in their mustaches. And of course by that time we all knew what it was. It wasn't the end of the world. We all survived.

**Margaret McCracken (Mrs. J. M.) Morgan, Tulsa, Oklahoma:** [*Synopsis of a phone conversation in Tulsa.*] Friends were visiting when a cloud bank in the northwest was sighted. Her father was milking cows in the barn. Her mother told her to tell Daddy to come to the house. When she went to the barn to tell him, he merely replied, "I'll be there in a little while." She said, "Right now!" Once aroused, the father looked at the cloud, saw the apparent danger, and told her to "RUN!" as he looked over his shoulder. The family all crowded into the root cellar, but just before going into the cellar she looked up and saw that the sky was beautiful. Then it was suddenly "godawful"—like an atom bomb—little mushrooms, "poof, poof, poof" just ahead of the storm. Her father opened the cellar door once and reported that the house was still there. [The possibility of the storm being a tornado probably caused the remark.] All during the storm, the family heard noises of things blowing around. One neighbor told them it was probably "the end of the world." But the most unusual aspect of the storm for Mrs. Morgan was the memory of her father's excitement since he was normally a slow-moving and unexcitable person.

   The next day everything was the same color: red dirt everywhere.

**Mrs. J. M. McCracken, Pampa, Texas:** [*Mother of Mrs. Morgan, adding to the story of Mr. McCracken in the barn milking. Synopsis of a phone conversation.*] "I told him, 'If you don't come right now, you'll be sorry!' When he did come into the house, he had covered the milk buckets with wet cloths, but the milk was black and had to be thrown out." The walls of the house (as well as the floors) were black. Because they had no electricity, it was necessary for them to buy many brushes from the Fuller Brush man to clean up the mess. To a Dust Bowl housewife, the vacuum cleaner was the world's greatest invention. The cleanup after the great storm was much like that after a flood: everything had to be taken out of the house and washed. The dust could not be merely wiped off because it stuck to surfaces rather than simply lay on them. Their house, like most of the others she knew of, was very poorly built. "It leaked at every seam, and there were seams all over."

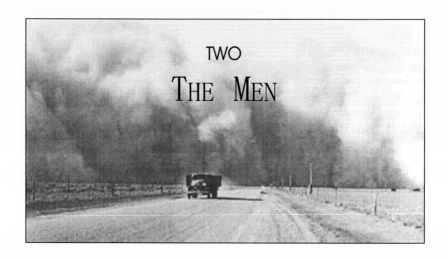

TWO

# THE MEN

Although women led hard lives, men in the Dust Bowl era were also faced with the major problems of keeping a family clothed, fed, and housed. Farming was a terrible task in drought and dust storms as crops failed year after year. Jobs were scarce, and the depression years forced men to find ways not only to provide for families but to shelter them from the terrors of such storms as that of April 14, 1935—the Black Blizzard, as it was called by some. A few of the following stories are humorous, more so than those told by the women; yet even in the midst of the humor there are expressions of fear and worry.

**Joe Shelton (ninety-three years old) and Charles Shelton (son), Pampa, Texas:** *Joe:* Black duster. . . . Oh, boy, that was a bugger. That was a humdinger. We had been down in Oklahoma visiting over Saturday night and you know that come up on Sunday. And we's coming back here trying to leave a little late, you know, in the afternoon, oh, I guess probably about 3 o'clock, and part of the road was dirt for about ten miles and the folks right in front of us was driving kind of slow and I drove around them, and when I drove around them they was looking back up here [*gestures toward his back*] and I hadn't noticed that thing, and I looked up there to see what they was looking at and I seen what they was looking at. . . . I told my wife, I says, "Look at that . . . north." And she hadn't seen it either. From there on, I had me . . . I'd bought me a new V-8 Ford, . . . and from there on I patted that thing on the back. When I got on the pavement I let the hammer down, too, and we got home just ahead of it. That was all. Just a very few minutes. . . .

*Q: It wouldn't have been something to be driving in?*

Oh, well, you couldn't have drove. You couldn't see nowhere. You couldn't see across the room outside. It just come a-rollin' in, you know, just like the end of time. By the way, I wondered whether the houses would stand up under the pressure and all, but they did. I don't think any of them blew down.

*Q: But I bet they were dirty.*

Oh, man, the inside of our house. We had a fairly new house, too, . . . but it didn't keep the dirt out. We had lights like that, hanging down, you know, from the ceiling, and it's kind of, oh, they was just pale and gloomy. You could see how to get around, all right, but I'd of hated to read a paper. . . .

We come up Red Deer Canyon. They'd built that highway about a year before and it was a good nice highway. That just saved our hide, 'cause if we hadn't had a good road and a good car, we wouldn't've made it.

*Q: I wonder if they stopped what they would have done.*

Well, they couldn't see how to drive. And I guess pretty soon, chances are their motor died, you know, 'cause that dust was awful. It was a-foggin' everything. It was penetratin' too. . . .

Thinking about that storm, we went up visiting some folks back up in Quincy, Illinois. We taken some pictures and showed 'em to these people . . . and that old boy, I remember the way he looked at 'em. He'd look at that picture and then he'd look up at me. . . . He couldn't hardly believe that. That same day they had a kind of dust storm up there, except they thought it was pretty bad. But said, he told me it didn't look like that. But I don't think he . . . I don't think he could hardly believe the dust. If I hadn't had a picture, he wouldn't have believed.

*Charles:* I was riding in the back seat. First time I knew something was wrong . . . Dad's not a fast driver and suddenly that Ford just jumped ahead. My sis and I were riding back there, and finally we looked out the back window and saw why. . . . Momma run out of gas the next morning when she backed out of the driveway. We got that close. I think she got up to the first filling station and run out of gas. We couldn't've went much farther. . . .

I had some rabbits and I had an old quilt and went out to put it over them. You know there was birds just ahead of that, wasn't there? Birds just, like, just tumbling and swooping around right ahead of it.

Some drunk—you might remember this—went up on the front steps of the Methodist Church. He thought the world was coming to an end. Of course, they always somebody comes out with a story something like that, whether it happens or not.

**Ben Guill, Pampa, Texas:** [Though not in school at West Texas Normal College at that time], I still went down to Canyon a lot because I still had so many friends there. And on the way, I went by and picked up a young lady by the name of Sarah Moore. We went up old 66 to get to Alanreed and noticed this low lying cloud over on the horizon, way off in the distance. And we were some miles from Alanreed at the time. So we kept watching and thought, "Oh, boy, it might rain." This thing kept building and building and getting bigger and bigger, and we saw it was just something. . . . It looked like it was an old black norther—blue norther that we used to have—it was just moving in. And it kept coming closer and closer. And so it was not a cloud but just a rolling mountain of dust. And we . . . it was just uncanny, and we didn't know what to do, but we were just trying to get to Alanreed real fast. And before you get to Alanreed, you got to turn . . . north off of 66 and you go down into a canyon— Alanreed's located in a canyon—so by this time this thing was rather terrifying. We didn't know what to expect, but we just went into this . . . just as we went down into the canyon, this thing rolled over us, and it looked as if we were going into a great cavern. And we didn't know what to think. We were young enough that we didn't particularly worry too much, but we went down and this thing just totally covered us like a blanket. So I turned on the lights, but we couldn't see. The headlights wouldn't penetrate. So we were on the side of this dirt road going into the canyon and we just sat there. Conversation, of course I don't remember that. But we sat there and it was just so weird and eerie. This blackness . . . the headlights wouldn't even penetrate it. It was very quiet except for the dust raining on the car. You'd just hear patter . . . I mean not just *s-h-h-h-h-t*. It was that thick. And it came into the car . . . everything. Of course, you couldn't breathe too well. We put handkerchiefs over our noses. And . . . just weird. So after about, oh, I'd say twenty minutes it began to be just a shade light just like the dawn only really . . . I really don't know how to describe it, really. A black filter light. A silver streak. It had silver through it a little bit. So I started up the car then began to pick up a little bit of distance in front of the car, and we just kind of went on very slowly. Finally got down into Alanreed and took her to the place where she was boarding. . . . That was the granddaddy of them all.

[*See Mr. Guill's description of his writing the one-act play "Dust" in Chapter Six.*]

**Dean Smith, Liberal, Kansas:** What was I doing on that Black Sunday? I was thumbing a ride . . . I'd been to Shawnee, Oklahoma, looking for a job. And I was thumbing a ride, and I picked up a ride with a deputy sheriff from Alva that his family was in Alva. The wife and kids were going to school, and he was deputy sheriff in Beaver County. Great big fella. We was motoring along there . . . he was driving along there in that Buick, you know, and said—this cloud commenced to roll in, you know— and he said, "Well, looks like this is it." Says, "Are you ready?" But the funny part of that . . . we stopped, of course, you couldn't see. There was a car stopped off the road, off of 64 highway, which did have some pavement on it at the time. . . . And before the darkness hit, there was a lady school teacher in this car, and we just talked a minute, you know, and we crawled back in our car, and she was in her little Model A Ford coupe, and this deputy sheriff says, "Now . . . it's gonna get pretty black." Well, it already started to get pretty dark. Says, "Don't try to go until we can all go." There was cars ahead of her. We had our headlights on, all the light you could get. And we could not see . . . there was a car pulled up behind us and we could not see their headlights in the darkness of that storm. It was terrific.

I didn't get home that night. I stopped at Farben. This guy lived right out south here off of 83, this deputy sheriff did. And he let me out at Farben and I had friends there and I went and stayed all night with them. And the next morning, I believe that there was a good half an inch of dust in their house on everything—I mean beds, ever' place. It was just that much dust come in.

*Q: Do you remember anything that your wife said when you got home—about that storm?*

She said . . . yeah, I know what she said. She said, "Did you find a job?" And I had. So just after that Black Sunday we moved to Shawnee, Oklahoma, and I sold tires for a few weeks, and I went to work for Montgomery Ward and sold washing machines and appliances to Indians.

That black blizzard was not as bad as it was to be without . . . a year or two without ever bringing in any money at all.

**Leon Daugherty, Pampa, Texas:** [*From a letter.*] I was raised in the small town of Hoover, Tx, which is 10 miles east of Pampa on the Santa Fè Ry. April 14 my father, Marvin Daugherty, was down to the little store he operated. My brothers and I were playing marbles. It was a beautiful day and still as a mouse. About 2 P.M. I looked to the north and saw a huge black cloud that extended across the horizon. I thought it was going to rain so I ran to tell my mother, Twila, that we should get the little chickens in their pens. My mother had on an apron and bonnet and began to scoop up the little chicks. She was putting them in her apron. Finally, the darkness was overhead, but the wind and dust hadn't reached us on the ground yet. I caught my mother by the arm and said, "Come on before we get wet." My brother and sisters had already gone to the cellar at my uncle's place about 100 yds away. But before we could get to the cellar door the wind hit. We couldn't see a thing. My youngest sister, Vera, started screaming; otherwise my mother and I would not have found the cellar door on our hands and knees. Seemed like the storm lasted about 3 hours. When we emerged from the cellar the sky was hazy and the air full of dust. On our kitchen table we measured 3/4 inch of fine dust. Some of our chickens had been blown about a mile away into Red Deer Creek. I have never seen such a severe storm since and hope I never will.

**R.C. Grider, Pampa, Texas:** I worked for Carl Benefiel at the Lanora Theater at night. And when the storm hit I had just gotten off taking tickets at the box office to go home to eat and come back. I was off from five to seven, and of course the storm hit, you know. Visibility was so poor that they just stopped the film. Static electricity in that air. When the storm first hit . . . I forget who was taking tickets . . . but the air conditioning vents . . . it just looked like fire came out. The smoke . . . you know the dirt in the air was . . . the booth in the back of the theater, the projection booth, it looked like fire coming out of those air ducts.

Carl Benefiel was the manager, and he had just recently bought a movie camera . . . it was the same size that they show for [movies]. He went out north of town and Skeet Gregory was with him, and Carl set up his camera and his tripod and shot pictures of it coming in. . . . Skeet said you just couldn't see a thing. They was out in the country.

[*No movies of the storm have surfaced as far as I have been able to determine.—F.S.*]

**Travis Lively, Sr., Pampa, Texas:** That was a Sunday. I had a brother who lived in Lefors at the time, and after church we went down there and had dinner with them and visited a while and came back. And as we came back into town, we could see that thing building up back there. My kids . . . didn't go with us to Lefors—there was something at the church—I forget what it was—and they were down there when we got in home. And frankly, I think you can tell by that picture there [*shows picture of storm approaching Pampa*], if you saw that thing approaching, it was kind of scary, and a lot of people just got almost panicked about it. Well, anyhow, we were dumb enough in those days— you know, you didn't always lock all your doors, especially in the spring or summer. You didn't think about somebody . . . I guess we didn't have anything that anybody would want. But anyhow, we went off and left it. And when we got back, why, one of the doors was open. And this is the absolute truth, I'll take an oath to this—I scraped the dust out of our living room with a hoe. I know that sounds unreasonable, but then that was actually a fact.

And then I got to wondering about the kids—where they were and how they would get home. So I got in the car . . . and went down to the church and the little coots weren't there. I guess they'd sent 'em home. Well, then I went on around to the

*This could be the picture Mr. Lively points to (page 45) as being one that "if you saw that thing approaching, it was kind of scary, and a lot of people got almost panicked about it."*

—Courtesy of Maxine Hawkins

[hardware] store, and I was wondering how everything would be in there, if there was anything we had that should be unplugged (we had radios). And this thing I do remember very well. Somebody drove up in front of the store there on Cuyler and Kingsmill and parked and they had their lights on. And I walked up to the front door, and so help me there were times when I couldn't see the lights on that car. It was just that dense . . . up above the cloud it had been a beautiful beautiful Sunday afternoon until that thing hit. And it just came rolling in, just rolling in, rolling in. I do remember people's comments, especially people who were newcomers here that day. They didn't know but what Armageddon was right on top of them. . . . [But] well, those of us who had been in some sand storms before, why, we just cussed it to be the big one and let it go.

**Jesse Mays, Pampa, Texas:** I was driving a truck between here and Pueblo [Colorado]. I was hauling in beer from a brewery up there. . . . Would you like to know exactly my recollections of that dust storm? . . . I can remember it as well as if it was yesterday. Then, the beer joints were open on Sunday, you know. See, repeal didn't come 'til '33, and you know Texas didn't get it 'til '34. I believe in September. Of course, now, this Sunday afternoon you're talking about. This fellow I was working for . . . his name was Sam Dunn . . . you may not remember it, but they had a packing house out on Alcott. And that's where we kept the keg beer. And then well, see, there was a Town Bar where the old . . . it's right across from the Rose Building, right there on the alley . . . that's where the first post office was in Pampa. Well, that's what it was when I come here. And there was a confectionery, they had one there. . . . Do you remember where the Chevrolet garage was? Well, the Elks Club was over it. And, you know, it was just you might say a professional gambling house. Which a lot of the Elks was. Well, see, I worked for him. And Sundays, why, I stayed up there and we kept the keg beer, see, out here at the packing house. So I got a call to deliver a keg of beer to the Town Bar. What time did that hit? Seem, to me it was about three or four o'clock in the afternoon. . . . Yeah, I think it was between four and five. Well, anyway, I left the Elks Club there, went out to the packing house, and I got this keg of beer and coming back, there

*Any person wandering around the Schneider Hotel (left) in Pampa, Texas, on the afternoon of April 14, 1935, should have considered running, not walking, toward the hotel for cover. That mass of dirt was probably less than a minute away from turning late afternoon into midnight. Mr. Benefiel, with his movie camera, ran to a place where he thought he could get some moving pictures, but the storm hit before he could get his camera set up. (See page 45.)*

—F. L. Stallings, Sr.

at the Worley Hospital I looked . . . you could see that. You could see it just as . . . oh, man, it . . . well, it was just . . . of course I'd been in it for two years driving between. . . . I went through the worst part of it between here and Pueblo—twice a week. I didn't pay no attention to it. So I go ahead and deliver this keg of beer and went on back to the Elks Club, and somebody called me to the phone. Well, they had a little phone booth in there, just like a regular phone booth, you know. Of course, the lodge was all going. They was playing poker in the next room. But I come . . . I talked to . . . I don't remember who it was. I guess it was somebody wanting another keg of beer. Anyway, when I come out, you couldn't see nothing. The lights was all on. It was pitch dark. Of course, a lot of people told you about it, you know. There wasn't no wind and there wasn't no nothing. It just settled and it stayed there. I guess it was after dark, you know, before it. . . . I imagine some of that dust went in that bank vault at the First National Bank.

Oh, and that night we had to take the bedspread off the bed and shake the dust off. I imagine that much dust on the table . . . on the kitchen table [*shows the depth with his hand*]. [Even if houses had been better built], that stuff would have gone through anything. [We had a lot of bad ones, but . . .] Oh, sure, man, man, man. Of course that was one that most people remember because there was no warning in that. There wasn't no sound. Seems like it was just like . . . it floated in just like a balloon coming—a big balloon. All that stuff, that dust come from southeastern Colorado and Kansas and the Oklahoma Panhandle. That's where it accumulated. It started up there, I imagine about Lamar. . . . Of course, as far as you could see was that just . . . that stuff was just a-rollin' in. Didn't seem like it was movin'. Just like a big tent, and when it hit, it was just like a big tent went over town. The lights was on, but you couldn't see nothin'.

**Mr. and Mrs. Dudley Steele, Pampa, Texas:** *Mrs. Steele:* We went to Lefors that day. If I remember right, it was a very sunny day, wasn't it? Didn't other people say it started out a pretty day? And everybody was glad that, you know, we were not having a dust storm. Then this one came up. And we were in Lefors, and I think we went riding, horseback riding.

*Mr. Steele:* I'm not sure we went riding.

*Mrs.:* Well, that's really not important. I think we did. Then we started home, started back to Pampa, and we were on the highway. And . . . Dudley, why don't you take it from there and describe what it looked like to you.

[*FS: 'Cause you were driving right toward it.*]

*Mr.:* Yes, we were driving right toward it. And, oh, I don't know. I'd estimate this wall would be somewhere in the neighborhood of five or six hundred feet high, maybe more. Kind of hard to tell if you look off in the distance. But it was just a black rolling lump as far as you could see it coming at you. It didn't have much distinguishing features at first, but as it got closer you could see the boiling mass of dirt that was in it. We kept coming, and finally we met. The wall and us in the car met. It was as light as this. I would guess it was five to six o'clock in the evening. At least it was plenty light, and when it hit it just turned night, completely dark—the sun went out. I guess we put a handkerchief over our nose or something.

*Mrs.:* I think I had a scarf, and Dudley said to me, "Tie the scarf over your face." And then he took his handkerchief and tied it.

*Mr.:* Just pulled off the road out there.

*Mrs.:* We couldn't see, so we had no choice.

*Mr.:* I guess we were four, five, or six miles from town, out where you make the turn there. We just pulled off and sat there, and boy, it shook that car. And that dirt went right through it. . . . It was shaking. We didn't know what was going on. Oh, I knew it was a big old duster. I'd never seen a black one like that. But we'd been having dusters for, what, two years? Had dust storms, but you know, they'd just be a big pall come in. Well, as I say, we sat there and finally the wind subsided, and things settled like a pall. But it never got light again. Darkness hit before . . . we never saw the sun again. I'm sure we didn't get home before it got dark. Then it was quiet. And then this pall of dust just settled over everything. We we just came home after the big rush stopped. . . . We finally . . . I tried a couple of times. As I remember, the lights wouldn't project very far because the dust was too thick, and I had to wait until I could see far enough with the lights. And as soon as it thinned enough—and I say thinned because you could still see that dust all the time—when it thinned enough that we could drive, and I drove on in I guess probably 15 or 20 miles an hour the rest of the way to town. It was just like driving in a fog, only the fog was dust. But that was it 'til the next morning.

*Mrs.:* I was teaching dancing at the time, and so the next day—I didn't have to teach Monday morning—it took me all morning to get the studio to where I could get the children in that afternoon. But they all came and all told different stories about what happened to them and what they thought about it, and so on. But I don't remember anybody was particularly excited. I guess they were children, and . . . they knew the sun would shine sometime, so they didn't worry about it. . . . And Dudley had to clean out the lab. He's a chemical engineer, and so liked to keep the lab spotless, so he had to go out and clean that—dig out all the dust. Of course, when you mopped or you put water on it, you had mud. He had mud in his lab.

**Dr. R.M. Bellamy, Pampa, Texas:** I'll tell you what I was doing. I had my wife and children, boy and girl, in the car, and I was making a house call to a fellow who was a taxi driver here. And he was, I was in the house . . . and he had pneumonia, by the way. Can't even think of his name anymore. But while I was in there, my wife came to the door, rapped on it and said, "Come out quickly!" And she said, "Look over in the northwest!" And she says, "What in the world is that? Looks like smoke. Big. Maybe a prairie fire." I says, "It couldn't be a prairie fire. It couldn't put out that much smoke." And none of us knew what it was. And we just stood there. And I said, "Well, I've got to finish with this patient," and I went back in the house and was out in a few minutes. And so we just sat there in the car watching that thing slowly rolling, not knowing really what it was. We'd never seen anything like that. And when it got close enough that we could see what it was, we turned around and headed for home right away. And got home and my wife closed all the windows, and we wondered what in the world can we do. It was just choking you. And I says, "The poor fellow with pneumonia. I don't know what it's gonna do to him." But anyway, we finally decided—of course, there was no air conditioning. We didn't have any in those days. And there was a movie house, the

Lanora. And they was supposed to have some kind of air conditioning. It was primitive, but it was some. We decided the thing to do, the best place to go is go down there and maybe that'll get out some of this. So we did. And I don't know how long we were down there, but a lot of other people were there for the same reason, I guess. Anyway, every once in a while somebody would report on it, you know, "It's kind of calming down." But that's what I was doing at the time it rolled in. Never saw anything like it before.

[*See discussion of "dust pneumonia" with Dr. Bellamy, p. 149.*]

**Ernest Baird, Pampa, Texas:** Well, sir, it was a Sunday afternoon, and my brother-in-law and my wife now (I married two sisters; I lost my first wife, the mother of these children.) We were living right over here at the Clayton Floral place, and it was a pretty Sunday afternoon. I had two daughters, and they was just kiddos, and at that time, you went to the country and got your milk, and I'm sure you've heard of T.C. Neal. The sun was shining as pretty as I ever saw, and we got in the car, my brother-in-law and his wife and me and my wife, and we drove out the Borger road and across the Humble [oil] camp and was a-goin' down by Mr. Neal's out by here at the Charlie Barrett place just a mile south, and pick up half a gallon of sweet milk. And when I crossed that track and looked back over there [*gestures*], that cloud was a-rollin' in. And I would say it happened between 5:30 and 6:00 . . . And my daughters was supposed to go to the picture show and then go on from there to the First Baptist Church to the Union, which met about 6:00. All right. When we got our milk, Mr. Neal told us to hurry home 'cause that storm was a-comin', and we looked and we got over here on Foster as far as what I called then the old Sawyer place, right along in there where I.S. Jameson used to live. It was a lead-colored, shingled, pretty good house. . . . And there we had to shut down right agin the curb. You couldn't see your hand before you. It was dark as pitch. And we sat there, I guess, fifteen or twenty minutes. And I run in low gear along the curb and got down to the Clayton place. Then the next thing come up: my son was at the house, oldest son, Clyde, and he hadn't seen the girls. Well, we worried about them, you know, where they's at. And knowed that storm

*From the looks of what seems to be rising in the background, one would hope the people living in the house did not need to use their privy very soon. They might not have been able to find it once the dust hit.*

hit, and they's supposed to be on the road to church. Well, we went to huntin' them, and went up to the theater, and went up to the church, and come back, and Mr. and Mrs. Harris lived just on this side of the street from us. Kathryn Harris and my girls run together. So them kids was safe and all right, right there in that house, right at us, hollerin' distance, and so it got pretty chilly and cold. The next morning, why, we had to sweep the dirt out with a broom and a scoop. And it cleared away then and that's just about all I know about it, 'member about it.

**Jim Dunn, Liberal, Kansas:** [*Probably combining the storm of Monday, April 1, 1935 (a real omen) and the April 14 storm. The spring of 1935 was probably the dustiest on record, though it would be hard to prove that, but March and April that year did have dust storms on at least twenty-six days, according to some who were interviewed during 1982 and 1983.*]

The reason I remember it, this was the first one that I had ever encountered. And this neighbor boy, who still makes his home in the same house in Garden City, and I were inseparable. We were repairing a Model T that we owned. We'd drive it one day a week and then repair it six days a week. And we were across the street in a barn where we shedded the thing. Had been working on it. Came home from school. School at that time was out about 3:00. And we were home from school and had been working laboriously in the garage, hadn't paid any attention to the exterior. Came out and noticed our mothers and lots of other of the housewives standing in the street looking up to the north. That particular time it looked like the doggonedest prairie fire that was imaginable. You could see little flecks of white against this particular pall of what we thought was smoke. And it was just rolling is what it amounted to, very much akin to what smoke would be. It was almost a still day. The breeze was practically nil. It was early spring, that much I do remember. And very nice weather—in fact, it was shirt-sleeve weather. But everyone was standing out looking at this great pall of smoke—supposedly— rolling. And this was probably 4:30, maybe 5:00. And these little flecks of which turned out to be birds, as the thing got closer. They looked like pieces of paper. And the skies were just as blue. All the rest of the horizon was just as clear as a bell.

When that thing hit, it was just like somebody turned the light off at midnight. And this boy's father had a retail store downtown, and we lived about six blocks from his store. He had walked it, come home at noon, then after lunch would walk back. When this thing hit, it was just automatically midnight. He called his wife and told her that he was starting home and she said, "I don't know whether you could make it or not." He'd been doing this over a great number of years, so it should have been almost rote. He started home, and the further he got, the more disoriented he became. He got down on his hands and knees, and was feeling along for the edge of the sidewalk until he'd hit a spot that there was no sidewalk and went over to the curb and did the same thing. Was crawling hands and knees there. And wound up—this was in the north-central part of the town. He wound up some place clear on the west edge of town which was complete disorientation. He couldn't see street lights. He couldn't see anything. The only thing he finally saw when it eased sufficiently was a dim glimmer of someone who'd left a porch light on. In one of those momentary times that the stuff abated slightly, crawled up on the porch, knocked on the door, and they did have a telephone. He called his wife, and he said, "I'm completely disoriented. I know where I am, but how I got here I don't know." She said, "Stay there until it clears enough you can get home." Well, that was some time the next day.

And I remember full well that particular storm because my father had come home from the bank at that particular point and he immediately started laying cold, wet . . . not cold but wet towels in all the windows to try to absorb the dust that was blowing through—I'm sure—the panes. That wasn't doing any good, so we got out the sealing tape, this old gummed brown package tape, and taped every doggoned one of the split sashes and around the whole windows. It did a pretty good job, but you had to constantly take a wet towel and keep the dust out.

**Fred Vanderberg, Sr., Pampa, Texas:** In '35 was the granddaddy of all dusters. I was just a kid, and right up here on the edge of highway 70 a man ran a little dairy farm up there by the name of Grady Enochs. And his son and I had gone across a little draw there to the big long shed to milk those cows. As we were walk-

*Although these photos were shot near Groom, Texas, and not from the position described by Fred Vanderberg in Chapter Two, it might convey a sense of how he saw the approaching storm and why he responded as he did to what he saw: ". . . it was a very frightening experience because I looked back and just right down here a mile or two it looked just like a black wall . . . And it was just a-rollin', just like a big ol' ocean."*

—Smith Photos, Pampa, Texas (Collection of F. L. Stallings, Sr.)

ing across there, Mr. Enochs, this man . . . father of this good friend that I was over there spending the night with, he says, "My gosh," said, "Look up there in the north," said, "My gosh that's gonna be a bad storm comin'." Well, I looked over in the north and I could just see a little red ring, kind of, just a little high not very much a-showin'. I says, "Oh, that's nothing, Mr. Enochs, that isn't gonna be anything." He says, "No," said, "that's gonna be a bad sucker over there." He says, "I can tell."

Well, we went across the draw and went to milking those cows, and for some reason—I'll never know what prompted me, but I'd got through milking several of the cows—I walked out and he had an old 15-30 tractor parked out in the lot, in the corral, to grind feed on, and I crawled up on top of this old tractor and looked back to the north above that barn. And it was a very frightening experience because I looked back and just right down here a mile or two it looked like a black wall. Didn't look to me over 100 feet in the air. And it was just a-rollin', just like a big ol' ocean, waves just a-rollin' and you could see it. It was just a-tumblin'. And I thought, "My gosh, is that the world coming to an end or what is that?" And I called to Mr. Enochs, and I said, "Come here, Mr. Enochs, and look at this thing!" And he came and stood up on the tractor with me, and he said, "My gosh, Fred," he said, "I believe that's just a wall of dirt." Well, we went up and sat down underneath that shed. There was no wind in this thing, just a complete wall of dirt.

And we sat there underneath that shed, and it turned just as black as jet. You couldn't see your hand in front of your face, and no wind, and I can remember Mr. Enochs struck a match— he smoked Bull Durham cigarettes and he had rolled him one in the dark—and sat there with that match and lit it and then he held that match up to each one of our faces, and where we had licked our lips it looked just white, you know, just like if you had made us up to be in a colored minstrel or something. Our eyes were white, but it just covered us, that dirt did.

Well, we tried our best to get back to the house with that milk, and it began to lighten up just a little bit. Well, we took that milk back to the house. And those people . . . it was back during the depression and it was terrible hard to make a living, and they counted on that milk. They made butter all the time and sold butter. He separated the cream from the milk with an old-fashioned turn separator, you know. Well, he tried to strain that milk in there, and no way did they ever get that milk clean. They strained it, I know, probably a dozen times, trying to get that dirt out of that milk. Finally they just threw it away. Couldn't ever get it clean enough to turn the separator on it.

But in the house then, his daughter and wife, they were going around, had a dish towel tied over their face, and they'd wet it to breathe. And they was a-coughin', and a-snortin' around there. And I never did have a dish towel over my face, but those two women did, and they were really coughin'. And the house, you could just barely see in that house with their little lamps, kerosene lamps, burning. You just couldn't see anything hardly but that stuff.

But after it was over with in the next morning, that dust and dirt, it looked to be a half-inch thick on the floor all over. They had to mop and run water and everything for a day or two to get that house cleaned up where that you wouldn't smell that dirt. It was terrible.

*Q: Do you remember how your mother and father felt, or any of your other people?*

Well, my mother and dad and my two brothers were living over there, and my mother said she thought the world was coming to an end because of that dark thing and the sky being blotted out and everything. But my daddy told her, no, that that wasn't biblical, that that wasn't the way the world would end, and he says there's no way the world's going to end in darkness that way. He says, "The Bible don't describe that," and he gave her some biblical quotations, so kind of straightened her out on her thinking. But a lot of people would look at that . . . I did. I said, "My gosh, Mr. Enochs, is the world coming to an end?"

It was a terrible thing to see. I'll tell you right now, that thing just rolled. It just *rolled* coming in. But my grandmother, Mrs. Myrtle Davidson Jackson [*see her journal entry, p. 27*], lived back over here on the edge of the breaks. And my uncle had just brought his team in from the field. He had a . . . about a 110-acre field right there by the house that he was cultivating feed. And working four head of horses and a couple of mules. And he'd just gotten in to the barn to take the harness off these animals. And when that storm hit, it surprised him so, but the thing I remember about him telling about it was Old Pete, a mule he had, he just went to braying. And if you've ever heard a mule bray, it's something to listen to. This old mule would bray every day at noon, just about ten minutes till twelve. If you were working him in the field, he'd bray, and he never missed it. He wouldn't be a minute off. That was a sign he wanted to go to the house. Well, he didn't bray in the evening. But Uncle Moore told us that when that storm hit that day, that Old Pete let out the loudest bray he'd ever heard in his life, and said that it was just like a cry of anguish that he was left out because it was some unnatural kind of a phenomenon that was happening to him.

**Sherman Harriman, Canyon, Texas:** I have a second-hand story that my wife has told many, many times. During this dust storm she was seven years old and she had an English bulldog, and as you know English bulldogs frequently have trouble breathing, and they had to keep someone up twenty-four hours a day for three days in order to keep a wet cloth across that English bulldog's nose because he was literally suffocating. And to go outside when he went outside to go to the bathroom, it took two people to go out—one to hold the cloth and one to hold the dog.

**James S. Kone, Canyon, Texas:** I was up in Moore County about that time, and I was operating a gasoline plant up there—running tour [*he pronounced it tower, meaning shift*], and about 2:00 in the afternoon I looked up and here this thing was coming in from the north. I don't recall anything about having any wet rags or having any masks or anything. . . . The thing came in and I almost blew up the gasoline plant up there because of the fact that we had a fire during the time the storm was raging. I don't recall it being as wild as the way . . . you know, the way it was blowing as a lot of others. This was more or less a floating type of thing that came in. . . . I don't recall having to spend the night out at this plant, but I do remember going back into the boxcar that I was living in—and we did have a construction boxcar, this fellow and I did. And you know how thick a nickel is—a pretty thick coin—and the dust was so deep and thick on top of this

James S. Kone, working in a gas plant in Dumas, Texas, might have noticed that in a few seconds he would no longer be able to see the school building that was about to be obliterated by the rolling dirt.

dresser that you could hardly see a nickel lying up there. . . . I know back in that period that they did come out with respirators or breathers, that you could wear, but ordinarily (just like every other contraption you have) it was at home when you needed it because you didn't run around with it hanging on your belt.

**Bob Gordon, Pampa, Texas:** We were in Mobeetie [Texas] at the time of the storm. The house, an L-shaped frame structure, was arranged so that the protected side was opposite the direction of the storm. The chickens in the "L" apparently thought it was night because they were walking around in a circle, one following the next but getting nowhere. A friend, P. Claude Ledrick, thought he'd gone blind because the storm turned the world dark so suddenly.

**Russell (Rusty) Neef, Pampa, Texas:** [*Unrecorded remarks taken down in a notebook.*] Halfway between Skellytown and Borger in the '33 Chevrolet when someone mentioned a "black something or other in the north." Mother told Dad, "We ought to get home" (a "shotgun shack") some miles away. They had just started toward home when the storm hit. The car headlights were no use at all. It was worse than black night because no light could penetrate. The father saw a house down the road with half a dozen cars in front. They stopped and went in and tried to fend off the dust with wet sheets and hankies. The bare bulb hanging in the middle of the room did very little good in lighting the room because the room was full of dust. After an hour or an hour and a half, the family decided to head toward home. Then, when they finally did get there and went into the house, they discovered "sand running off the window sills" like little waterfalls. The lemon chiffon pie the mother had left was "black as the ace of spades." The children (Rusty was seven) were covered with sheets, but it was already too late for them to do much good.

The next day everything and everyone was covered with dirt. They first used a scoop shovel to start the cleanup, and for a week afterward were still trying to get rid of the dirt.

[*One reason they couldn't finish the job was that dust blew every day during the following week, according to several people.*]

**Jack Osborne, Pampa, Texas:** [*Synopsis of interview at Neef welding shop.*] Ten years old at the time of the storm, in Perryton, Texas. His mother lit the lamps (kerosene), but they didn't help, even in the house. Wet cloths over their faces also didn't help very much. They tried to cover the dishes on the table, but the dust got into everything. The dirt was so thick in the house after the storm they used a shovel to get some of it out.

**Ollie Dunivee, Miami, Texas:** Remembers asking his father, "Daddy, do you know how to pray?" Also remembers people standing in front of the Lanora Theater (in Pampa) so they could feel the cool air coming out. [*It was probably the only air-conditioned building in town at the time.*] The people in front of the theater were probably not there during the storm.

**Edwin Nelson, Pampa, Texas:** [*Phone interview synopsis.*] Lived on a farm south of Pampa, started there in 1920. Remembers the cloud rolling. Neighbor drove 70 miles an hour to stay ahead of the storm, but other neighbors parked in the bar ditch and sat through it in their cars in front of the house. "You couldn't see your hand in front of your face." The family went into the basement, where they could hear the wind. He called it a black norther.

**Orville Christopher, Miami, Texas:** [*Synopsis of unrecorded interview.*] The storm rolled in from the north, "so black you couldn't see nothing." And there's been "nothing like it before or since." He and some friends were at the Gulf station and when the storm came he turned the lights on, "but you couldn't see 'em. I had to feel around to find the lights. I stayed at the station until time to close, but after while it started to lighten up. . . . We sold as much pop as we did gas because they had to have something to wash the dust down. The boy in the gas station across the street didn't know what to do. He closed and then opened and closed and opened." A lady who lived about a block from the station, whose husband was at the station watching the storm with Christopher, sent her son over to the station to tell the husband to get home. He didn't pay any attention, so she came herself. She was very excited and scared, but the husband just told her,

"It's just a big dust storm, the worst you'll ever see." It was the granddaddy of 'em all, he said. It came rolling in like a ball, like a head rise on a creek. It was black as tar, black as the inside of a mule's mouth. He mostly watched the storm from inside Ellis Locke's car parked in the gas station driveway.

**Ben Ezell, Canadian, Texas:** [*Synopsis of interview at his office.*] In 1935 was working for the Post in Quitaque (Texas). His main memory of the storm was that it filled the press and every piece of machinery in the office with dirt, and all the ink in the building had to be thrown out. He couldn't see and couldn't breathe.

[*Anyone familiar with print shops can imagine trying to clean dust from ink rollers, from all the gears and cams in a linotype machine, from type cases with hundreds of pieces of type—not to mention the usual things such as the floors, window sills, and supplies of paper.*]

**Harold Hudson, Perryton, Texas:** [*Synopsis of interview at his office.*] Was twelve years old in 1935. Told of a man and his wife in a new Buick on a trip from Chicago. Got caught in the storm on their way from Liberal, Kansas, to Amarillo. [*See his reminiscence on pp. 110-112.*]

**Fontaine Cooley, Guymon, Oklahoma:** [*Interview not taped; a synopsis follows.*] Nine years old, living in Moreland, near Woodward, when the storm hit. The yard around the house was bare, and the wind throwing the dirt against the house made it sound like someone throwing gravel at the house. Afterward, you could touch a bush and create another dust storm. Brothers—thirty-five and sixteen—died five days apart that summer from dust pneumonia. Remembers that the static electricity was so bad they could not work on the windmill [*because of metal blades on the mill fan*]. He remembered seeing but did not know where to find bottles of "Genuine 1935 Rolling Duster Dust" that sold for a quarter.

**Wilbur Wells, Guymon, Oklahoma:** [*Interview not taped; synopsis follows.*] Was working for the paper at the time. The storm was probably the most severe and certainly the most dramatic, but it was probably the least destructive and least to fear. It was the same with all rollers: "You couldn't avoid a sense of fear because they towered high and they were black, and there was not a breath of wind, and they rolled." This one was rolling and was black as could be. There was nothing to do but stand and watch it. There was a gradual increase in wind, but it died and then the dirt just fell. [*He wondered aloud if maybe the wind might have been stronger as one rose in the air, causing much the same effect as a person rolling a barrel by pushing it at the top with his hands.*] To those sitting in the house, the dust seemed to penetrate right through the windows and walls. Even in the best of houses there seemed no way to keep it out. Wells insisted that the 1935 storm was not as bad as some in 1938.

**Lawrence Balzer, Hooker, Oklahoma:** [*Synopsis of unrecorded interview.*] On April 14, 1935, the family had a gathering, the kids were playing, when someone noticed a bank in the northwest that "doesn't look like a rainstorm." The kids were gathered up and herded into the house and when the wind hit, it got *really dark*. Chickens roosted right where they were when the dust hit. Lots of people in the town were at a rabbit run over near Tyrone [*see Chapter Three*]. The dirt was like flour, so fine that it ran off the window sills like water. It also stuck to the walls. To clean out the house, they started with scoops.

He remembered that sometime in the early morning after the storm—about 1:00 or 2:00 A.M.—they heard a voice from outside and looked out to see a man who'd got lost in the storm and had seen the light in the house. He told them he thought he would have died if he hadn't found their house. He also remembered the dust on the bed the next morning.

**Bill Hutchinson, Lake Charles, Louisiana:** [*Phone interview synopsis.*] In Pampa, Texas, on Sunday, April 14, 1935, was downtown on Cuyler, at the Crystal Palace (ice cream and confectionery store) waiting for John, his brother. When the parents came, Bill got in the car but John was not to be found. Driving home, they nearly ran into John (visibility being about zero) on the road. He was totally covered with dirt.

**A. D. Kirk:** [*Copied from a document dated December 25, 1978, provided by Mrs. Faye Stowell of Pampa, Texas.*] The duster that I best

"A Kansas Dust Storm"

*Actually, Mr. Balzer said, this is a photo of Hooker, Oklahoma, another postcard proba-
bly sent to folks who had never seen any duster, much less a black one.*

—Courtesy of Maxine Hawkins

remember hit Pampa, Texas, in April 1935, on a Sunday afternoon. The weather was perfect—a warm, gentle, southerly
breeze, not a cloud in the sky. The air was clean and clear. One
could see to the horizon in all directions. It was a day for people
to be outside, and they were out in large numbers—playing tennis, golf, and doing things they most enjoyed. I drove out to the
little air strip where a barnstormer was taking people up for
rides. While sitting there in my car, I noticed a low dark line of
what I first thought was a cloud along the northern horizon. It
made no sense. There was not a cloud in the sky. As I watched,
it got taller and spread from the west to the east horizon. The
black mass was coming on fast. The duster hit when I was a half
a block from home.

This duster was unusual in many respects. The wind must
have started picking up dust in Canada and continued picking
up dirt and dust across North Dakota, South Dakota, Nebraska,
Kansas, and Oklahoma. The front of the cloud was a rolling,
tumbling, boiling mass of dust and dirt about two hundred feet
high, almost vertical, and as black as an angus bull. There was no
dust in the air above it or in front of it. It came across the prairie
like a two-hundred-foot-high tidal wave, pushed along by a sixty-
mile-per-hour wind. When it got to a house or power pole or any
other object, the house or whatever disappeared. It was weird.
After the front passed, the darkness rivaled the darkness inside a
whale resting on the bottom of the ocean at midnight.

Most of the dust storms were local in character. The wind
would come first and as it increased in velocity it would pick up
dust and gradually get worse. The one that hit Pampa that
Sunday was entirely different.

People who watched it coming saw something that they had
never seen before and may never see again. I watched it from
the time it appeared on the horizon until it ungulfed [*sic*] me in
darkness. As it approached it was awesome, majestic, fearsome
and fascinating. There were many stories about people after it
was over. A shift worker who had been asleep was getting dressed
to go to work. Sitting on the bed, he had one shoe on and was
reaching for the other one when the duster hit his house. He
thought he had suddenly gone blind. The preacher, holding afternoon service, was preaching the gospel when the duster hit

the church. Some people in the congregation thought it was the end of the world.

Oh, yes, I got home okay. I parked my car against the curb and, holding a handkerchief over my nose and mouth, I felt my way along the curb to the driveway and finally found the door.

**Clyde (Bud) Hodges, Miami, Texas:** [*From a letter.*] The black dust storm that came in on April 14, 1935, was the Daddy of them all, there has never been another one like it. People who didn't have a radio thought the world was coming to an end when it rolled in.

There was a family who run a dairy south of us and north of Hoover a couple miles on Bob Campbell's place[,] they had a barn that was built half under the ground, anyway the[y] milked all these cows by hand and had to start milking early in the evening. This storm came in very quite [*sic*] the wind was rite [*sic*] on the ground, as it closed in on him everything went black and he thought he had gone blind as you could not see . . . your hand in front of your face.

Even the birds were scared, they were flying in front of the cloud by the millions.

We were at Canadian, Texas that day, my parents lived there, my mother [had] gone to a country singing near the Okla. line and had started home, when they saw it, they thought the world was coming to an end, and got out of car and got in the ditch, scared to death, they could not drive for several hours because you could not even see the front of your car, the traffic stopped ever where.

I had a hired hand here at home and he crawled under the bed, scared to death.

I had a neighbor who was bringing a truck load of cattle at the time. This guy cussed every breath, I ask a hired hand who was with him what he done when the cloud come in. He said he quit cussing.

My father had a radio that told us it was coming, but none [*sic*] one thought it would be like that. The wind didn't blow real hard, but it was all on the ground.

I have seen that year the dust would blow every day for a

week at a time, I have even seen a pasture blow, the grass died out as big as ten acres in spots. You know something good comes of about every thing, before that time our pasture had a lot of what we called red grass, a big bunch type, but cattle wouldn't eat it if they had anything else. Anyway, next spring the rains came, and the pastures waved with winter grass in those dead spots, the kind like you have in wheat fields. A lot of people said it would ruin the pasture, cattle got fat on it and when it died in June, little bufflo [*sic*] and mesquite grass came up in it and that fall and up to now we have a better grade of grass than we ever had. That grass seed had blown in with the dust storms.

The dust came in the houses then about 1/4" per day, of course our houses wasn't as good as they are now.

The dirty thirties brought people closer together, they had time to help each other and be a good neighbor. God would say good came out of it.

THREE

# THE RABBIT DRIVE

At least half a dozen of those interviewed for this study mentioned the Tyrone rabbit drive, also known as a rabbit run. Only two provided enough detail to make it appropriate to dedicate a chapter to that event.

Jackrabbits searching for food caused enormous damage to young crops of wheat and feed grains, leading farmers and others to try to limit the damage by driving the rabbits before a line of men wielding clubs. As the line moved toward a chicken-wire trap, the rabbits would be clubbed to death. It was probably not the kind of afternoon activity enjoyed by most people, but when crops were being destroyed (in almost the same way grasshoppers and locusts destroyed crops), any method was better than losing whatever could be grown in the midst of drought. The rabbits also provided food for families.

A photograph of the rabbit drive was published in the *New York Times* in 1986, continuing the link between the event and the Black Sunday storm.

**Noel Southern, Pampa, Texas:** [*A rabbit drive near Tyrone, Oklahoma, was scheduled for Sunday, April 14, 1935. Before he talked about the dust storm, Mr. Southern explained the way such a drive is conducted.*] The way they do that is a whole bunch of people gather and they will put up a fence at a certain place. Then these people will go and spread out and start from a place, maybe two miles

69

from the spot where the fence is, and on this particular day we had started from the south walking north to the fence. I don't fully, exactly remember whether it was two miles that we covered—two sections—or not. But we did walk in. And they have clubs. They don't use any guns. . . . They just have a . . . maybe a hard stick, different things, of course to use, or limb off a tree or something like that. A baseball bat is too big. You want something you can hit quicker. And that is an experience, if you ever have the opportunity, don't miss it. I would. I would drive a hundred miles.

The people that drove cars that wasn't making the drive—maybe wives or something or another—and parked their cars up here by the fence, and here, just about the time we got within a . . . well, of course we could see it when we got an eighth of a mile down there—rollin' up there. Just like that [*gesture: hand over hand*]. In other words, oil-pool smoke—you know how smoke just rolls. That's the way this cloud looked. And Edna says here they went to the cellar; they thought the end of the world was coming. Anyway . . . that's my wife, Edna . . . we just kept on and kept on. And lo and behold, just as we got 'em up there within you might say fifty steps before the fence, and the rabbits running everywhere, here that thing hit. And it was so black . . . I did . . . before it got so bad I couldn't see at all . . . I run and got in a car with somebody, and I put my hand up like that and you couldn't no more see it than nothing. It was just as black as any night you've ever experienced.

I would guess it lasted probably forty-five minutes or an hour. Then it got to where it lightened up and enough that you could see how to manipulate. Well, these people that I was with—I guess it was some of my wife's folks because I rode in the car with them down to her uncle's place about a mile and a half from where the rabbit drive was.

I forget now whether that was the time it got pretty cold afterwards or not. Seems like it did—got pretty cold afterwards. But I wouldn't be sure about that. [*See the article by Randall Bensch, p. 116.*]

**Dr. Lewis Armstrong and Betty Williams, Liberal, Kansas:** [*In a conversation during an interview session they talked about rabbit drives with some mention of the Tyrone event but also about some of the* *brutality that was deemed inappropriate for children, and perhaps women, too.*]

*Q: I was just reading in some of the old newspapers that they've got back here (in the Liberal Public Library), that some rabbit runs were canceled because of the dirt. There was one down at Tyrone, and there must have been a hundred people out there caught by that storm.*

*B.W.:* They thought God was punishing 'em. . . . Justly thought God was punishing 'em, too, for profaning the Sabbath.

*L.A.:* They had a rabbit drive?

*B.W.:* I remember that.

*L.A.:* I remember going on one, but not on that particular Sunday.

*B.W.:* Yeah, I knew there was one over at Tyrone.

*Q: But there were stories in this paper—funny stories—about . . . they kept canceling this one because of the dirt. When they finally had the thing, they were expecting several hundred people and they were going to do a tremendous area. I've forgotten how many sections* [square miles] *they were going to cover. They were expecting to get 50,000 rabbits; they got 1,500.*

*L.A.:* That's quite a few rabbits.

*B.W.:* We just went on one of those. And of course it takes a whole lot of people— start walking, walking, walking. So us kids were allowed to do the walking, but when they'd get 'em in to a little fence thing and start clubbing 'em, and the folks wouldn't let us watch that. I could see 'em jumping in the air from where we were. You'd see one make a high leap and I could see one jump in the air, and I could see a club come down. Folks wouldn't let us watch 'em kill 'em.

*L.A.:* Oh, they wouldn't?

*B.W.:* I don't think I would have wanted to, really.

*Q: I think it's sort of with mixed emotions that that sort of thing happens.*

*B.W.:* I think it's still mixed emotions. After that (killing so many rabbits) then the coyotes got real bad, and so then we lost all of our chickens.

*Q: Oh, they did notice that they got two coyotes along with their 1,500 rabbits.*

*B.S.:* Hmm, two coyotes. Been funny if they'd got a skunk or two.

**Maxine Browne and Mr. and Mrs. Delmer Webb, Liberal, Kansas:** [*In another conversation about the big storm, the Tyrone rabbit run is discussed after an exchange about the birds that also were mentioned in many interviews.*]

*M.B.:* We've often wondered what happened to those birds and those pigeons that flew ahead of the storm.

*Mrs.W.:* I imagine they suffocated.

*M.B.:* They went ahead of the storm. They weren't in the storm; they were ahead of it.

*Mrs.W.:* They could have flown over the top of it.

*M.B.:* But they didn't come back. They didn't come back.

*Mrs.W.:* Yeah, they didn't want any part of it.

*M.B.:* I think we had those trade winds: We traded dirt with Nebraska one time, and then we traded with Oklahoma and Texas the next time.

*D.W.:* I don't recall seeing any dead birds in particular. . . . We were having a rabbit drive. It was northwest of Tyrone.

*Mrs.W.:* I wasn't, but he was.

*D.W.:* [Even as the storm got closer to the rabbit drive] we didn't quit. We stayed right out there.

*Mrs.W.:* The main part apparently wasn't there, then, because they couldn't see anything.

*Q: I don't know how they did. How could you see?*

*D.W.:* We just walked. We were almost to the pens, so we just stayed . . . got down on our hands and knees and got 'em on in. Then we started hunting for the cars, which you couldn't see. We had a pretty good idea of where the cars were, of course, up close to the pens. I was down there with Mr. Norton in a Model T.

*Q: How many people were out there? Do you have any idea?*

*Mrs.W.:* A lot of people. My dad and brother were there.

*I.K.:* I saw a picture of it. . . . Wouldn't you say there were about twenty there?

*D.W.:* People? Closer to two-hundred.

*I.K.:* Oh, is that right?

*D.W.:* See, they string you out for a mile. I would guess we were strung out a mile and a half, probably, to start with, down on the south side. Then, of course, when you get closer, why, you get consolidated where you're just standing one right beside the other. But I imagine there was two hundred people in there.

**James Lambuth Hague, Dallas, Oregon:** [*From a letter.*] A friend in Hooker, Oklahoma sent me the newspaper clippings of the 50th anniversary of "Black Sunday."

I lived in Tyrone, Oklahoma at that time and I remember "Black Sunday," April 14, 1935. I participated in the "Rabbit Hunt."

It gave me a scary feeling as I watched the dust storm roll in. I knew it wasn't the end of the world as we'd had several dust storms preceding "Black Sunday." I'd seen it rain mudballs following a dust storm and the rain would clear the air.

Several men were riding horses, directing the rabbit drive. The thing that impressed me most was how the horses laid down to get away from the storm so they could breath [*sic*].

My younger brother, David, got dust pneumonia and the Dr. told my dad to get this boy out of the dust bowl.

I have a picture of my family leaving Tyrone with my Dad and Mother and eleven of their twelve children. Five of the younger children rode in the open trailer along with the bedding, clothes and cooking utensils, as they headed for Oregon.

[*The following article, probably published in a Liberal, Kansas, newspaper sometime in May 1986, led to a bit of sleuthing. The picture referred to of the Tyrone rabbit drive has been published many times— mostly in the area where the black storm occurred—but no one interviewed for this book identified any of the people in the picture. (See next page.) So this story meant that we had to find the date of the publication in* The New York Times. *The clues in the letter meant that what had to be done was to find the correct Mother's Day during the 1980s (assumed because the letter does refer to "a 50-year-old" photo) and copy whatever in the article is relevant to this collection of reminiscences. The picture as published in* The Times *was not very clear on the microfilm and was cropped so that the dust storm does not show. The "Editor's Note" at the end of the letter was in the Liberal paper.*]*

### Tyrone Rabbit Drive Makes N.Y. Times
*Dudley Acton, 320 South College, Mountain Home, Ark.*

Enclosed is an article that I think will be of interest to people in your area.

When our daughter, Janet, who lives in New York City,

*Rabbits menacing crops were being chased and killed (to be used for food) on Sunday, April 14, 1935, near Tyrone, Oklahoma. At the climactic point in the hunt, just as the rabbits were being cornered, the storm struck and ended that day's hunt.*

—Photo by Paul Cherry, Tyrone, Oklahoma; Courtesy of Noel Southern, Pampa, Texas called home on Mother's Day, she said she also wanted to talk to Daddy. I was just "floored" as she told me that that morning's issue of the *New York Times* had a picture of the 1935 dust storm over Tyrone, Okla., and a related story on the front page of the business section.

She also added that she was sure she remembered seeing the same picture at home. We do have an original print of the photo here at home as our family lived in Tyrone at that time, and some of them are in the picture. I quickly found my copy of it and we had a great time pointing out people and items of interest in it.

Anyway, when my relatives make the New York Times, my friends are going to know about it! That picture was the rabbit drive northwest of Tyrone on the famous Black Sunday of April 14, 1935. My mother, Mary Acton, and my grandmother Durham are standing on the running board of my folks' 1929 Pontiac. Mrs. Clifford Parham is standing in front of them. Richard Locke is in the rumble seat of Locke's Ford roadster. I think I also recognize Dewey Frain and Asa Hearne in it.

My wife and my mother and I had recently returned from a week's visit with friends and relatives in Liberal, Tyrone, Baker, Beaver and Hooker, and attended the Tyrone reunion over Easter weekend. We were still recalling it when the N.Y. Times article was printed, so it was of special timely interest to us.

The following day, Janet called and talked to the man who had written the story for the New York paper. He told her that the same picture had also been run in their paper in 1935 and that much of the story had come from their Houston office.

He said he was looking for something to emphasize the hard times in Oklahoma [in 1986] and found the picture in their microfilm library, although it had little to do with their present problems. He was also very surprised at the coincidence of a New York City resident seeing her grandmother and great-grandmother in a 50-year-old Tyrone, Oklahoma, picture in their paper.

Editor's Note: *The New York Times* news story headlined "Desperation Descends on Oklahoma Once Again" [*the "Once Again" does not appear in the microfilm copy used here*] sets forth how the oil and farm slump has brought on a new depression and that

Dust Bowl memories haunt the state. The only picture pertaining to this area is the 1935 Tyrone dust storm photo, which is surrounded by present-day pictures of farmers and oilmen who have lost farms and businesses—primarily concentrated in an area from Enid to Woodward.

Only one part of the *Times* article has anything to say about the 1930s storm. After discussing how a couple, Mr. and Mrs. Troy Ogden, had struggled against the 1980s "bust," the story continues:

### Desolation Descends on Oklahoma
(New York Times, *May 11, 1986*)

Mr. Ogden's mother, Cleo Ogden of Woodward, still has vivid memories of the Depression. She grew up on a farm near Shattuck, in the heart of the Dust Bowl. She still remembers that "Black Sunday" in 1935 or 1936 when the worst dust storm of all rolled in: "It came at 4 P.M., like a tumbleweed rolling over the hill, black as coal. The wind blew so hard. When we came out the dirt was piled up on the buildings like snow banks."

But she stayed, married Ernest Ogden and together they worked hard and built a successful retail liquor business, Southway Liquors. The business rode the oil boom to tremendous highs. "Business was fantastic—we made a heck of a good living," Mrs. Ogden said. The couple sold their store to their son, Troy, in 1982, and since then business has been cut in half. "This is the worst time since the Depression—I've never seen it this bad," says Mrs. Ogden. . . .

[*The following verse was printed in the* Guymon Daily Herald *Pioneer Edition, April 13–14, 1985. It is reprinted here by permission of the No Man's Land Museum in Guymon. It is a fitting end to the chapter, reflecting—fifty years later—some of the sentiments of those who were witnesses to the rabbit drive.*]

### The Rabbit Drive
By Jennie Mouser

We lived in the Dust Bowl and Depression Days,
And the weather had its part to play.
We tried to raise some feed and grain.
To keep our animals alive was our big main.

It was so dry and the rabbits were thick.
To get rid of them we needed a trick.
They ate a lot of our feed and grain,
So to have a rabbit drive was our gain.

We went to the sand hills for the big drive,
Which took place, April fourteenth, nineteen thirty-five.
It was an unusual calm and beautiful day.
And a big crowd gathered from miles away.
The excitement was all around.
To get the rabbits, they all were bound!

They had made a huge wire pen
To drive all the rabbits in.
There were hundreds of rabbits in that drive,
And none of them were to stay alive.

They should have sensed the warning that day.
As the black storm cloud was headed their way.
But all that mattered and filled their minds
Was the number of rabbits they'd get this time.

When they got the rabbits to the edge of the pen,
The storm hit fast and the screaming began.
It was so black, blacker than any night.
My, it was a horrible sight!

It folded over us like a wave.
The dust was so thick we couldn't breathe,
And we wondered what to us it would lead.
We began to think this might be the end,
And we had no time to make amends.

They threw down their clubs and sticks and stones,
It seemed as if each one was all alone.
Women and children were crying and praying then
That they could just be with their families again.

Then the wind started to blow,
And some of the dark clouds started to go,
And a little daylight we began to see
So everyone could get where they needed to be.

Now I never did mind to see a rabbit shot,
As I always thought it was part of their lot,
But I thought they should be given a chance some way
For some of them to get away.

And now I would like to have my say
About the rabbit drive that day.
I think an Upper Hand was waved
And all those rabbits' lives were saved!

# FOUR
# NEWSPAPER REPORTS, APRIL 1935

Newspapers throughout the area of the Black Blizzard carried headlines and long accounts of the coming of the storm, its presence, and its eventual settling. In addition, the stories included bits of humor, some obvious lore that became fact in later telling about the storm. But there were also firsthand accounts of reporters who had been caught by that duster and were awed and frightened by what they had just experienced. Most of the newspaper articles reflected on the reasons such a storm might have occurred and even what might be done to prevent such phenomena in the future. Some articles have been edited somewhat due to the length of the originals.

The first two articles, which appeared in newspapers prior to the big storm, indicate just how severe the spring of 1935 had been even before April 14.

### Immensity of Dust Storms
(*Amarillo Daily News*, April 1, 1935, p. 4)

If you have wondered just how much earth was moved in the recent western dust storm, you might be interested in the estimate submitted by A. F. Turner of Kansas State College.

Mr. Turner says that if a 96-mile line of 1 1/2-ton trucks could be put to work hauling 10 loads apiece daily, it would take them a year to haul back to western Kansas the dirt that was

*The site of this photo is said to be Logan, Oklahoma, in some newspapers and Goodwell, Oklahoma, in the paper cited below.*

—Courtesy of *Amarillo News-Globe*, April 13, 1975

blown over to the eastern half of the state. Altogether, he says, there would be 46,520,000 truckloads to be moved.

Putting the thing in that form helps us to realize the terrible destructiveness of the storm. You don't need to use your imagination very hard to understand that a lot of good farm land must have been ruined to provide those 46,520,000 truck loads.

*After weeks of dust since the first of March, the following humorous "prayer" was answered by the storm that was to become the most remembered one of all.*

### Dusty Dust Doth Distress Direfully
(Southwest Tribune, *Liberal, Kansas, April 11, 1935, p. 2*)

Here is a lamentation which is appearing in a number of exchanges, and the credit is given to "Exchange." We publish it for the reason that it describes some features of the dusty period, even if the prayer part is not true to form:

"Kansas Prayer"

"Oh, Lord, the pioneer spirit has had about all it can stand! We've put up with Indians and grasshoppers and depression and Democrats without bothering you too much about it, but these dust storms are going to drive us crazy.

"After we've worked all day long cleaning and scrubbing and mopping and sweating, and our hands feel like they've had a lye bath, then wake up in the morning and find that it has to be done all over again—well, Lord, it really is a little discouraging.

"This is the seventh day of it now, and if we don't get rain before long there's going to be the greatest migration of history —the Kansans are going to move out! It's driving women to drink and strong men to tears. Our hair is covered with dust, and we can feel it grinding between our teeth. It's ruined our complexion and our business, our homes and our highways, and it's darned near ruined our dispositions.

"If we stay at home a film of dust settles on our glasses so we can't read; it's all over the food and the bed clothes; we can't take a bath because the tub is full of Kansas, Colorado, and Oklahoma. If we do take a bath, we're covered with New Mexico, Texas, and Nebraska before we can get dry!

"If we go outdoors it's worse—the wind blows so hard we can scarcely stand up against it. We can't drive a car any place because we can't see the radiator from the driver's seat. We can't walk because the wind tears us to pieces. Anyway, there's no place to go except where there's more dust and we've had plenty. We're in a heck of a fix!

"Now, Lord, we've tried to behave ourselves even though we do live in Kansas—we've gone to church and paid our tithes and done most of the things you want us to do, but if you don't send us a nice big rain pretty soon, there will be a lot of Kansans whose faces you will never see in the next world. And some of 'em do say that the region below will be a haven of rest after the 'Black Blizzard' days they have endured in Kansas."

### 'Worst' Duster Whirls Across Panhandle
(Amarillo Daily News, *April 15, 1935*)

———

Farmers Pray
For Rain But
Wind Answers

———

Norther Strikes Sunday To
Blot Out Sun, Turn Day
Into Night

———

Kansas Governor Says Soil
Undamaged; Storm Hits
South Texas

(By the Associated Press)

North winds whipped dust of the drought area to a new fury Sunday and old timers said the storm was the worst they'd seen.

Farmers prayed through dust-filmed lips for rain.

A black duster—sun-blotting cloud banks—raced over Southwest Kansas, the Texas and Oklahoma Panhandles, and foggy haze spread about other parts of the southwest.

Easter [Palm Sunday?] services at Lindsborg, Kansas, opening with a chorus singing "The Messiah," were carried on in dust-laden air.

Pilot Injured.

Worshippers thronged the Methodist Episcopal Church of Guymon, Okla., to seek divine deliverance. Instead of rain, there came a deluge of dust which rolled and boiled like the smoke of a gigantic oil fire. Unable to beat the storm in a race for the Hutchinson, Kansas, Municipal Airport, Pilot A. L. Welty suffered a broken nose and possible internal injuries when his plane nosed over in a forced landing.

Dust and winds barred Leon McKinnon, parachute jumper, from attempting a descent from an airplane with home-made wings at Dallas, Texas.

Makes Record Trip.

The black duster made the 105 miles from Boise City, Okla., to Amarillo, Texas, in 1 hour 45 minutes. Hundreds of Sunday motorists lured to the highways by 90 degrees temperatures and crystal clear skies were caught by the storm.

Farmers and agricultural officials of the dust area, Kansas, Southeast Colorado, Northeastern New Mexico and the Texas and Oklahoma Panhandles, reported the soil was not damaged and that crops could still be made this season if it would rain. Governor Alf M. Landon of Kansas pointed out top soil ranges from 10 to 30 feet deep at many points in the area.

———

## STORM TURNS CITY
## INTO TOTAL DARKNESS

Blotting out every speck of light, the worst duststorm in the history of the Panhandle covered the entire region early last night.

The billowing black cloud struck Amarillo at 7:20 o'clock and visibility was zero for 12 minutes. Gradually it cleared and Weatherman H. T. Collman said the storm would be over by morning. The black, ominous cloud rolled over the Panhandle from the north, an awe-inspiring spectacle.

Into Central Texas

The storm continued southward and had moved into Wichita Falls by 9:45 o'clock, the Associated Press reported.

A large area west and southwest of Temple was reported

feeling effects of the duster, which moved onward into South Texas.

Warning of the terrible storm reached Amarillo about 45 minutes before it struck. It came from a woman at Stinnett.

The woman called Sheriff Bill Adams. He did not learn her name.

"I feel that your people of Amarillo should know of the terrible duststorm which has struck here and probably will hit Amarillo," the woman said. "I am sitting in my room and I cannot see the telephone."

### 8,000 Feet High

A gentle, north breeze preceded 8,000-feet-high clouds of dust.

As the midnight fog arrived, the streets were practically deserted. However, hundreds of people stood before their homes to watch the magnificent sight.

Darkness settled swiftly after the city had been enveloped in the stinking, stinging dust, carried by a 50-mile-an-hour wind. Despite closed windows and doors, the silt crept into buildings to deposit a dingy, gray film. Within two hours the dust was a quarter of an inch in thickness in homes and stores.

Reports from the north at 10:30 o'clock last night by the Santa Fe dispatcher said that the moon could be seen at Woodward, Okla., showing that the storm was clearing rapidly.

### Forecast Cloudy

The weather forecast for today was partly cloudy and colder.

The storm struck just before early twilight. All traffic was blocked and taxi companies reported that it was difficult to make calls for nearly 45 minutes. Street signal lights were invisible a few paces away. Lights in 10 and 12 story buildings could not be seen.

John L. McCarty, editor of the Dalhart Texan, of Dalhart, the center of the drouth-stricken area of the Panhandle, called a few minutes before the storm arrived in Amarillo.

The storm struck Dalhart about 85 minutes before it hit Amarillo and the city remained in total darkness for more than that length of time, he said.

### Couldn't See Light

"I went outside the house during the storm and could not see a lighted window of the house three feet away," Mr. Carty [*sic*] said.

Borger, Perryton and other cities on the North Plains reported similar conditions, proving that the storm was becoming less vicious the farther south it moved.

Damage to the wheat crop, already half ruined by drouth and wind, could not be learned last night, but several grainmen believed that the dust would cover even more of the crops.

The storm started yesterday when a high pressure area moved out of the Dakotas toward Wyoming, according to Mr. Collman.

Most of the dust was from western Kansas and Oklahoma, he said.

A new device for eliminating dust was one result of the storm.

A linotype operator, forced to stick to his post in a dusty shop, appeared with a narrow strip of shoe shining cloth, lined with sheepskin, tied close to his nostrils. When dampened, he said, it made breathing normal.

A Santa Fe train, scheduled to depart for the South Plains about 8 o'clock, was held up nearly an hour waiting for the dust to subside. With improved visibility by 11 o'clock it was reported making good time, aided by a strong "tailwind."

*The following article was provided by Mrs. Horace (Ruth) Brooks, White Deer, Texas.*

### Writer Caught in Dust
By Robert Geiger
(The Amarillo Daily News, *April 15, 1935*)

(EDITOR'S NOTE: Of all types of soil blowing, the black duster provides the most awe-inspiring manifestation of the power of the prairie wind. It moves with express train speed and blots out the sun so darkness prevails at midday. Such a storm was that which swept over part of the Southwest Sunday. An Associated Press correspondent caught in the cloud tells of the experience.)

BOISE CITY, Okla., April 14 (AP)—Old timers say it's the worst storm to hit this part of the country—dust ridden though they've been in recent weeks.

The cloud caught us, Staff Photographer Harry Eisenhard and I, on the highway about six miles north of town.

We first noticed it about nine miles out. Rain seemed to be coming. Then it resolved into a dust formation.

• • •

"What a swell picture," Harry said. We stopped at a knoll, took several pictures, then turned the car around for flight.

The great cloud of dust rose a thousand feet into the air, blue gray. In front of it were six or seven whirling columns of dust, drifting up like cigar smoke.

• • •

We went down the road about 60 miles an hour to keep ahead of it. We had seen an old couple at a dilapidated farm house, and stopped there to warn them, but they had already gone.

• • •

Speeding on, the car was suddenly engulfed by a flank movement of the cloud. Momentarily the road glimmered ahead like a ribbon of light in a tunnel, then the dust closed it. It became absolutely black as night. We slammed on the brakes and turned on the car lights. Exploring by touch, we found the car in a dust drift.

• • •

Backing out and keeping a door open to watch the edge of the highway, we took two hours to move the remaining six miles into Boise City.

En route we picked up Jack Atkins of Hunter, Colo., his wife and three children from their stalled car.

"Without doubt," said Atkins, "this is the worst blow that ever hit this section."

• • •

Undoubtedly hundreds of cars were stalled throughout the area by the dust, seemingly semi-solid in the darkness.

Lights can barely be seen across the street.

It took the storm just one hour 45 minutes to travel the 105 miles airline from Boise City to Amarillo, Texas.

• • •

The funeral procession of Mrs. Loumiza Lucas, en route from Boise City to Texhoma, Okla., was caught eight miles out and forced to turn back. Mrs. Lucas was the mother of Fred Lucas, well known Texhoma rancher, and E. W. Lucas of Boise City.

Half a dozen small boys and girls sought by police as missing were found to have been lost on the way from their home— they started when skies were clear—to a drug store.

### "Topics of Our City"
[*Column by Olin Hinkle*]
(Pampa Daily News, *April 15, 1935*)

Well, Sunday's duster will serve quite well as the "worst" until a better one comes along.

We regret we didn't see it approaching. Did any of you readers get a striking picture of it?

We hear that Pampa housewives are threatening to pack away all curtains and linens until the rains reduce the possibility of dust storms.

But we, now having to do much cleaning after them, are learning to get along with the dusters. Interesting aren't they(?)(!)

Musing of the moment: Dust is bad. Marauding Indians would be worse. Dust is bad. A flood would be worse. Dust is bad. A destructive tornado would be worse. Dust is bad. To live away from our oil resources would be worse. Dust is bad. An annihilating fire would be worse. Dust is bad. A war would be worse. Dust is bad. A lethal epidemic would be worse. Dust is bad. But the worst duster falls far short of being as bad as many other things which can befall a territory. We've got to do a bit of pioneering in rebuilding the soil of the southwest.

### Daylight Turned Into Inky Blackness as Duster Hits
(Pampa Daily News, *April 15, 1935*)

A whiskey-intoxicated man in north Pampa saw it and thought the world was coming to an end; he began hunting for a church and incidentally sobered up. . . . Some persons became hysterical. . . . A man who was dressing after a bath had put on one shoe; when he reached for the other, he could'nt [*sic*] see it, nor could he see his hand in front of him.

These were a few of the many stories that were being told today after the passage of one of the most magnificent and gigantic spectacles in the repertoire of the merciless Mother Nature. Wonderstruck citizens of this community were awed for 15 minutes yesterday before it bore gently but viciously down on them, choking them with dust and silt, turning the shank of a balmy afternoon into midnight blackness.

It came out of the northeast about 6:45 o'clock, almost an hour before sunset. When it was a half mile away, watchers could see that it was about 2 miles high. They could also see that if all the oil in the Panhandle had gone up in stupendous ebony-blue clouds of boiling, bollowing [*sic*] smoke, it would not have made a sight half as fearful. After it struck with a swishing, gritty noise, the darkness was complete. The atmosphere was inky for at least 20 minutes. The duster raged furiously until 10 o'clock when it began to subside, but the air was still full of dust until early today.

**Storm Climax**
Southwest was Plunged into Inky
Blackness Yesterday with Only
Few Minutes Warning
BROUGHT TERROR
Some People Thought the End
of the World was at Hand
when Every Trace of Daylight
was Obliterated at 4:00 P.M.

(*The Liberal News*, Liberal, Kansas, April 15, 1935)

A people who during the past two weeks thought they had experienced the worst that could come in the form of dirt storms, looked on in awe and many of them in terror yesterday afternoon when with only a few minutes warning a great black bank rolled in out of the northeast and in a twinkling when it struck Liberal plunged everything into inky blackness, worse than that on any midnight, when there is at least some starlight and outlines of objects can be seen.

When the storm struck it was impossible to see one's hand before his face even two inches away. And it was several minutes before any trace of daylight whatsoever returned.

The day up to that time had been one of the few pleasant ones of the past several weeks. There had been no wind and only a few hazy clouds in the sky. The temperature was unusually high and the day was one inviting people into the out of doors after day after day of dust.

Consequently, many were caught out in the storm which came so suddenly that few realized it was even on the way until it was right upon them.

### Describes Approaching Storm

One Liberal citizen who was a member of an outing party yesterday afternoon thus describes the approach of the storm: "We were out in a field hunting arrowheads and I had been watching the sky for I wanted to get a good picture and was paying particular attention to the few hazy clouds around.

"We had a full view of the sky and of the horizon in all directions. It was oppressively warm and scarcely a breeze was stirring. Suddenly as I looked to the north I saw a faint dark rim along the horizon. I thought at first it was a cloud like those which had been passing over to the southwest. Then I noticed the ragged edge at the upper edge of the dark rim.

"I called to another member of our party to look and it was so faint at that time she did not even discern the outline. We were only 16 miles from town and no one felt any apprehension but I suggested that we start home so in case a dust storm should be coming up we would get home safely before it struck.

### Descended at Unbelievable Speed

"We were more than the equivalent of two blocks from the car when I first noticed the haze in the north. We walked directly to the road where the car was parked and by the time we had reached it that great black bank was boiling against the horizon. Against an inky background there appeared to be hundreds of whirlwinds in a straight line, making a solid wall of slender white columns of dust against the background. We started the car immediately, driving east and before we had gone a mile we could see the great boiling cloud of dirt sweeping across the prairie from the north. It descended upon us and we stopped the car right where it hit us, not 20 minutes being elapsed from the time I first sighted the slight haze in the distance.

"There were seven of us in the car and the darkness was so dense that we could not even see the form of the person sitting next to us. I was driving and could not even see the steering wheel in my hands. In fact I could not see my hand one inch from my face.

"We sat there awestricken in the most intense blackness we had ever experienced. Several minutes passed, then at last it lifted sufficiently we could see the radiator cap.

"There was a reddish hue over everything. Gradually it grew lighter and we could see the outline of the ditches at the sides of the road, although we could not see anything in front of us and when we turned on the car lights it made it all worse. They seemed to reflect right back to us from that swirling mass in which we were enveloped."

### People Became Panicky

The storm struck just as the funeral service for Lee Wilson was being concluded at the First Methodist Episcopal church. The church was filled for the service and the pall bearers, Eastern Star and Business and Professional Women, had just passed from the front door to the entrance steps when the black wall was seen descending. People gazed at it terror stricken. Some had children at home or at play somewhere and grew hysterical. Most of the people rushed back into the church building and Undertaker S. A. Miller warned the people not to leave the building. Many went to the church basement.

A great many people both in the country and in town, who had warning of the approaching storm before it hit, went to cellars or basements.

"I was alone in the house when it came," one Liberal lady said this morning, "and was so stunned by the sudden blackness that I just stood and gripped the door frame. I didn't even think of turning on the lights for a few minutes."

At one farm home northwest of Liberal one of the residents said this morning the dust and darkness was so thick that a match was lighted by one member of the family and the others could not see it across the room.

Many feared tragedies might occur in the storm from people smothering or being lost who were out in it, but thus far no reports of serious consequences have come in.

### Made Way by Fence

Ralph Davis, age 13, and Vilo Davis, age 9, had gone arrowhead hunting in a field some four miles west of the cemetery, northwest of Liberal and when they saw the storm approaching headed for the fence. When the storm struck them Ralph took hold of his sister's hand and with the other hand he followed the wire fence and they were able to get to shelter at a farm house about a half mile distant. His hand still bears the scratches from the barbs.

Their parents, Mr. and Mrs. Oscar Davis, were attending the Lee Wilson funeral and feeling alarm for their children's safety went out in the raging storm in search of them. Knowing just about where they had intended going they found them at the farm house.

Many people were caught out on highways, but most of them after sitting in their cars until the worst of the storm passed, were able to creep along at a slow pace, waiting at times for the dust clouds to break away sufficiently to see the dim outline of the ditch at the side of the road and reach home in safety.

### Take Pictures of Storm

Several people who had an unobstructed view of the approaching cloud took pictures of the storm and there should be some good ones. J. N. Maxwell lamented the fact this morning that a movie camera was not available for some pictures such as seen once in a lifetime could have been secured.

Radio reports were to the effect that the storm was bad all the way from Denver, Colorado, to Iowa. O. J. Wilkins tuned in on a radio report this morning that at 7:00 A.M. today the dust storm was just on the outskirts of San Antonio, Texas.

Engineer George Walker says the storm hit Dalhart, Texas, at 6:30 yesterday evening and that traffic was tied up for three hours.

The storm struck at Pratt at 3:30, but was not so bad at any time but that cars could travel although traveling was dangerous.

Bob Wilkins was north of Liberal when he saw the storm coming and drove between 50 and 55 miles an hour with it about 100 yards behind him and kept ahead of it that far.

### Has a Believe It or Not

Static electricity had been so strong during the recent dust storm that Louis Thompson, living five miles north and one mile east of Liberal, used it to run a small engine.

The electricity popped and snapped on the windmill wire giving Mr. Thompson an idea of using it for "juice" for the engine which needed a battery and coil.

It is hard to believe but Mr. Thompson says if any one wants to see it done just come out during some electric storm.

### Turn Porch Light On

"I was guided home during the storm yesterday afternoon by porch lights which people had thoughtfully turned on," one Liberal business man commented today. "I turned our porch light on so if anyone were out he could come and find shelter," a Liberal business woman says.

Turning on porch lights when a black dust cloud descends may guide someone to safety.

*From the same paper, this story was printed just under the previous article.*

### Two Boys Lost in Storm
#### Willard Bangs and Milton Leaming Say They Never Want Such an Experience Again

Willard Bangs and Milton Leaming had a bad experience during yesterday's storm, which struck them just as they were coming out of the breaks of the Cimarron river near the Earl Hirn land and they were lost for some time. The boys relate the following account of their storm experience:

"We just got out of the breaks of the Cimarron river, missed the road and got into the wheat fields. We drove in the field about two hours before finding a road. When we found a road we had lost our directions and didn't know where we were. We could just see the ditch with head out the window. The car began to miss on the account of electricity in the air. We couldn't see to drive onto Highway 83. We sat there about 10 minutes and then started driving down the road about 10 to 15 miles and [*sic*] hour and saw two red lights. The car started and went about 10 to 20 feet and went in the ditch. Thought it had turned over. We got out and tried to help them get out but it was useless. Then there was another came along and had a chain and pulled them out. Those in the car were from Hugoton.

"While we had been trying to get to town Millard had his handkerchief over his face to keep from choking down. We drove in to town and guessed at where the Eleventh street road should be. We had to roll down the window on Millard's side. Milton held his head out the window all the way to town. We went through an experience which we never want to go through with again if we can possibly help it."

*Beneath the story about the boys' adventure was the following.*

## Birds Ahead of Storm

Several people reported seeing flocks of birds ahead of the dirt storm yesterday, apparently trying to outfly the dirt cloud.

*(The following article was provided by Kay Wisnia, Western History/Genealogy Department, Denver Public Library.)*

## U.S. Sends 20,000 Men To Fight Dust As Worst Storm of Year Hits West

### Drifts Nine Feet High Piled Up By Wind on Road Near Durango

CCC Men to Be Sent to Stricken Region; All Southern Colorado Enveloped by Haze; No Immediate Relief in Sight

By Clyde Byers
(*The Denver Post,* April 15, 1935, pp. 1, 3)

———

Another blinding dust storm boiled over parts of five states like a scourge Monday. It affected all of southern Colorado from the eastern to the western boundaries, and inflicted heavy damage and real suffering in parts of New Mexico, Kansas, Oklahoma and Texas. Dust drifts nine feet high were blown up near Durango, Colo.

Alarmed by the situation, officials in Washington put the machinery of seven government departments in high gear to alleviate the distress and push programs designed to prevent recurrence of the stifling storms. Twenty thousand civilian conservation corps enrollees are to be sent into the stricken area to work on the latter programs and relief activities are to be broadened.

Monday's storm was continuation of one that swirled over Colorado and parts of Nebraska, Kansas and Oklahoma Sunday. The storm struck Denver at 2 P.M. Sunday and moved southward about four hours later. It blotted out the sun, blew up sand drifts that stopped trains and automobiles, and grounded airplanes. The gale-like winds tore down wires in Denver and filled homes and stores with a thick film of powdery dust.

Slight Prospects of Relief Seen
As Pall Hangs Over Five States.

The storm was the most severe of the series that started March 1 and have recurred with increasing frequency and intensity. In the area affected Monday there were slight prospects of relief, either from strong winds which might blow away the dust drifts or from rain which might settle them. . . .

Fiftieth 'Duster' in 104 Days

Oklahoma residents rushed for storm cellars when Sunday's "duster" appeared on the horizon. Perryton, Tex., was visited by the fiftieth duststorm in 104 days.

Temperatures tumbled quickly throut [*sic*] the vast area when Sunday's storm struck. The temperature in Denver at noon, according to official recordings of the United States weather bureau, was 71, but in two hours it fell twenty degrees. Later it slumped to 49 degrees. . . .

The storm generated sufficient static electricity to cripple automobile ignition systems and scores of motorists were temporarily stranded because the static was so intense. When the storm abated, they found they could start their engines again. At the height of the storm, motorists said, they received distinct electrical shocks when they touched door handles and similar attachments on their cars. Motorists made it a practice to drag wires and chains to ground the static and prevent short circuits. . . .

*The following story was provided by Mrs. Horace (Ruth) Brooks, of White Deer, Texas.*

### Black Blizzard is Described
### By News Writer Caught in It
(The Amarillo Daily News, *April 16, 1935*)

(Editor's Note: For two years dust has been transforming once fertile wheatlands of a region large as New England into desert. The United Press sent a staff correspondent into the region worst affected, to report first hand what he saw and what he learned from the inhabitants. His tour will carry him through the Oklahoma and Texas Panhandles, eastern New Mexico, southeastern Colorado, and western Kansas. The first dispatch follows.)

By Frank McNaughton
Copyright, 1935, United Press

CLAYTON, N.M., April 15, (U.P.)—That wall of dust, at least 10,000 feet high, boiled over the horizon on the wings of a gale and engulfed me and every animate and inanimate object to blackness laden with stinging dirt.

I drove here from Felt, Okla., through a region once called the "Bread Basket of America." The storm broke suddenly at about 5 P.M. yesterday. Leaving Felt I heard cries of "Dust storm, dust storm." I saw men and women and children running toward homes. Brave with inexperience, I drove on.

Soon the fearsome force was upon me. Across the horizon the earth rose into the sky. At the top of the dense black wall was a weird yellow fringe. I raced the storm for 55 miles, seeing the ground, like the troubled surface of a volcanic pool, rising into the air. It caught me at the M. H. Doersken ranch. I wheeled into the ranch yard and stopped six feet from the stout, tightly built stock barn. Before I could dash through the doors the dust hit. I spat on my handkerchief and held it to my nose. I could not see my hand at my face.

The dust was inescapable. It sifted through the double walls of the barn and made the air almost unbreathable. I(t) was like emery dust. My lungs still ache.

In the stalls, frightened cattle bellowed and snorted incessantly. Gradually the first phase of the storm passed. I opened a door and after a time could see the outline of the automobile. After two hours I could see the ranch house 60 feet away.

In the next few hours the storm thickened and thinned alternately several times. Between me and the sun the dust streaked over the plains in sheets. In an interval of light I saw a chicken's head protruding from a drift and pulled the bewildered bird free.

The remainder of the trip to Clayton was frightful. While in the barn two feet of dust had drifted against the car. Driving was by instinct. Once I ran into a ditch that had been filled with dust. Another time I ran over a farmer's mailbox which became visible only when it was a foot beyond the radiator cap.

It is not flippancy when I say I had received a taste of what R. A. Donaldson, L. M. Price, Preston Foreman, G. E. Stewart and others told me last week when I visited Stratford, Tex., east of here, after a swing from Sayre, Okla., through the Texas Panhandle cities of Amarillo and Dalhart.

### Caught on Lake
### in Dust Clouds

———

Sunday's Storm was Terrifying
Enough to People on Land but
Those Trapped on Lake Larrabee
Had Real Experience

———

(The Liberal News, *April 16, 1935*)

People with their feet on firm earth were terror stricken when

Sunday's storm struck, but imagine being out on Lake Larrabee in a boat! "How to Keep from Getting Old" is the manner in which Ralph St. Aubyn heads the following account of a group of Liberal fishermen who were trapped on the lake in the storm:

I thought that I had had close shaves, but I realize now that until last Sunday everything before have been mild affairs that had happened to me. I think I know somewhat the way a ship-wrecked sailor must feel tossing about in a small boat on heavy seas.

It all started very lovely with D. S. Parkinson and son, James Parkinson, Les Shelton and son, Bob, and I leaving for the lake Sunday morning to fish. The day was above par with just a thin haze of dust in the air. Upon arriving at the lake we secured boats. Mr. Parkinson and James in one boat and Les, Bob and I in another boat. Very little happened all morning; we didn't even have the fun of catching many fish.

All of us came back to the boathouse about 1 o'clock to eat a bit and went back out again on the lake in about 30 minutes. We had been having poor luck fishing down by the dam in the deep water, so we thought that we would try shallow water close to the north side. Les, Bob and I were about two hundred yards off of the point on the north side. Mr. Parkinson and James were west of us up to the neck of the lake.

### Blackness Descends

Along about 3:00 o'clock the wind went down and the lake was as smooth as glass. We glanced to the northeast pretty soon and here it came about a mile away. The anchor was pulled and we started to row. The great cloud of dust seemed to be rolling over and over as it came. The advance part of the cloud seemed to be about one hundred feet high; that part came over us for perhaps five seconds before the dust itself starting [*sic*] ingulfing [*sic*] us. By this time we were only about fifty yards from the north side, the last glimpse of land we had was some small trees. Then it got black and when I say black, I mean black.

### Water in Boat

We knew that we weren't far from shore so Les and I tried to row. All we could do was to try to go straight ahead against the wind. It was impossible to see each other in the boat. All that could be done was to yell at each other. We didn't seem to be getting anywhere rowing and didn't even know that we were going in the right direction, so we dropped anchor and tried to ride it awhile, but while this was being done the boat had gotten a little crossways of the wind and taken in a lot of water.

Well, there we were with anchors down and attempting to ride it out. By this time Bob, the boy was pretty frightened; as a matter of fact, we all were, but Les and I were too busy to think much about it. About this time the dust slacked up a little and from one end of the boat we could see some small trees just like the trees that had been our last sight of land before the storm hit.

### Lost in Water

I am telling you I didn't know that just a scrub cottonwood could look so good. Those trees were actually beautiful to see. We started toward the trees and were up to shallow water, so Les and I jumped out to pull the boat up on land and it turned dark again. We lost our direction and before we knew it we were in water waist deep. We had started out to deep water, so we felt our way back to shore and pulled the boat up on land as far as possible. By this time the boat was almost full of water. I never was so glad to stand on dry land in all my life.

### Couldn't See Ground

The sky cleared a little and we discovered that we were on the west bank of the lake, just opposite from where we thought we were. We walked around the dam and up to the lunch room, and couldn't even see the ground under our feet at times, but were well satisfied to know that solid ground was under our feet.

To the lunch room at last. Several people were already there and they were just waiting for people to report in that had been out in boats, and a real cheer of relief went up as we walked in. I doubt if anybody can picture the sight that we presented, after being soaked in water and then walking around the lake in the dust. And right here is where I want to pay tribute to Mr. and Mrs. Cooper, who are in charge of the boats and lunch room there. They sure handled the situation in splendid shape, getting blankets and dry clothes for the wet and cold people and starting a fire to get warm by.

## All Land Safely

Inside of an hour all the people who had been in boats reported in. It was a real miracle that somebody didn't get drowned. If any of the boats had been south enough to have washed against the cement instead of the west side, they would have broken the boat all to pieces and been real lucky to have gotten out alive.

The last that we had seen of Mr. Parkinson and James, they were just pulling anchor as the first of the dust hit. They were about twenty-five yards from the north shore. James says that he scorched the bottom of his boat he went to shore so fast. Just as the black hit, their boat touched the shore and James dug an oar in the sand and held till they could see a few feet and then got out to the land. They sat under the cliff on the north side and let the wind blow over them for awhile before starting back to the lunch room. James tells that he noticed a couple of prairie dogs go by while they were sitting there.

Among other Liberal people who were caught out in a boat were Dale Hubbard and Dr. Hatfield. By 10:00 o'clock it cleared a lot and we came on home, safe but I didn't know how sound, after a day of experience not to be forgotten. The next time that I am on the lake I am going to start for shore if I see a rain cloud five miles away.

## Tour Dust Area
### Governor Landon Heads a Group
### Surveying Damage in Western
### Kans. from Sweeping Storms
### VISIT FARMERS
### Government Man to Take Pictures
### of Conditions Back to Washing-
### ton as Proof of the Situation
### which can be best Explained

———

By the Associated Press
(The Liberal News, *April 16, 1935*)

TOPEKA, April 16—Governor Alf M. Landon last night headed an expedition of officials into the dust storm drouth sector of western Kansas intent on learning first-hand the extent of crop and damage.

With him were M. L. Wilson, an assistant secretary of agriculture, and Dean Harry Umberger, Professor W. E. Grimes and Professor R. I. Throckmorton, all of Kansas State College, Manhattan. Wilson came here from Washington, D. C., to start a survey of the dust storm menace in Kansas, Colorado, Oklahoma, Texas, and New Mexico.

The dust storms were laying low when the group set out in a motor car, but the Kansas chief executive laughingly expressed the hope one would start sweeping across the plains while they were in this area so that the Washington officials "could see what one is like."

The group planned to spend the night at Colby where they were to inspect soil erosion projects at a state experiment station. Today they planned to drive south through the western tier of counties, scene of the winter wheat crop devastation. They hoped to visit Garden City, Hugoton and Liberal. The latter two towns are in counties where the federal government plans to retire submarginal land.

They will talk with farmers in the region to obtain their ideas on what should be done in a long-time program to conquer dust storms.

### Another Dust Storm Likely
Wind From Southwest May
Become Higher Today,
Says Collman
(The Amarillo Daily News, *April 16, 1935*)

Velocity of the southwest wind today will increase sufficiently to cause another dust storm, H. T. Collman, meteorologist for the U. S. Weather Bureau here, reported last night after noting the low pressure area to the northeast.

After one of the worst dust storms in the history of the Panhandle had swept across the plains Sunday evening, the citizenry yesterday saw one of the pleasant days of the spring.

March had 20 dust storms and the first 15 days of April had 10.

## No Rain in Sight

There is no rain in sight for the Southwest, Mr. Collman said.

Stories of weird experiences in the storm Sunday night were circulated in Amarillo yesterday.

Murry Watts, photographer, was exhibiting pictures he had taken as the dust storm approached Sunday. Mr. Watts and Albert Bivins, rancher, went out Sunday morning to get some dust pictures and had their day climaxed when they were forced to spend the stormy night in the old two-story hotel building built by the XIT Ranch Company northwest of Dalhart many years ago. Watts had some excellent photographs of the billowing sand clouds.

## Girl Scouts Lost

A group of seven Girl Scouts, accompanied by Miss Harriet K. Walker, were lost in the canyons at Harding's Ranch during the storm.

L. F. Kirk, 1211 Jackson Street, had taken the group to the ranch. When they failed to meet him at the appointed place, he started to the ranch headquarters to telephone Amarillo for assistance. After his car stalled in the storm, he had to walk to the headquarters.

The girls and Miss Walker were found about midnight, but it was two hours before they could be reached and brought out from the deep canyon.

## Proved a Friend in Need
### E. G. Kindschi Braved Raging
### Dirt Storm to Aid Stranded Liberal Motorists
(The Liberal News, *April 18, 1935*)

Friendly acts of kindness always help to brighten the pathway, but in times like these they are as a real beacon light. People of the west have always been known for their open hospitality and readiness to extend a helping hand. That hospitality was put to a real test Sunday during the terrific storm, which was so out of the ordinary that many people actually wondered if the end of the world might come.

The way people over the county opened their homes to people trapped out in it is something which those who were privileged to experience that hospitality will never forget. E. G. Kindschi was one of those Good Samaritans.

A party of several Liberal people consisting of Mr. and Mrs. F. M. Baker and daughter, Goldie, Mr. and Mrs. Bert Long and Miss Maurine Long and Eugene Kindschi, caught by the storm, were stranded in a sand bed which the wind had carried and piled across the road from fence to fence but which they were unable to see in the swirling dust until they were stalled in it. The dirt was so bad that most of the time it was impossible to see the equivalent of a car length in any direction. To make matters worse, the static caused the motor to stall.

One of the men and boys in the party made their way by following along the fence line to the Kindschi home nearly a half mile distant. When appraised [*sic*] of the situation, Mr. Kindschi got Jack Edwards, who works for him, they went out in the raging storm, got Mr. Kindschi's truck and made it through the blinding dust to the stalled car which was towed to the Kindschi farm and placed in shelter. It was a bad night for anyone to be out, and Mr. Kindschi still has a weak limb from the bad fracture he received in the Armistice Day accident here in 1933. But he thought nothing of his own comfort in aiding the others in getting in to warmth and safety.

The seven people were welcomed as though they were paying guests at a big hotel and taken into the little home. Every housewife knows how the sand sifted in every crevice during the big storm. To prepare a meal for seven unexpected guests on the best of days would frustrate many a housekeeper, but Mrs. Edwards went quitely [*sic*] about removing the sand while the storm was still beating against the little house and in a short time had a hot meal ready.

The meal over, Mr. Kindschi, assisted by Mr. Edwards, made beds in an adjoining room for the stranded party, where they were made comfortable for the night. In the morning they arose to find a hot breakfast awaiting them. Mr. Kindschi and Mr. Edwards immediately set about endeavoring to get the car in operation and with the assistance of George Lee, who happened along and used wires to ground the static, this was at last accomplished and the party returned to Liberal. They will not soon forget the kindness of Mr. Kindschi and the others.

It was urgent that two members of the party get to town early in the morning for school and business, so they started out afoot down the road and when they had hitchhiked a mile and a quarter, Oren King came along and played the Good Samaritan again, taking them in, although he had a full load as it was, there being nine passengers in the car the most of the way into town.

There are no doubt many other instances of neighborly acts of kindness during Sunday's storm.

### Oil Floating
### In Dust Clouds
### Over Plains Area
(The Amarillo Daily News, *April 20, 1935, p. 1*)

TOPEKA, April 19 (AP)—There's oil floating around in the dust clouds that have tormented the great plains region in recent weeks.

Gov. Alf H. Landon, himself an oil man, told of examinations he made of dust deposits while on a tour of Western Kansas this week.

"Many residents in the affected area called my attention to the oily consistency of the dust. You could feel it by rubbing the dust between your fingers. The dust would leave an oily spot where it fell," he said.

Others have made similar observations.

The governor said he had no explanation for presents [*sic*] of the oil. He pointed out, however, that oil wells dot much of the plains region in Southern Kansas, Oklahoma and Texas.

"However, the entire plains territory has been considered potentially rich in oil and gas," the chief executive said. "This oily character of the dust may be new proof of that theory."

### Black Blizzard
### Declared 'Worst'
### By Judge Hoover
(The Amarillo Daily News, *April 20, 1935, p. 10*)

"I give up—Sunday was the worst—"

Judge H. E. Hoover, pioneer Canadian banker, lawyer and

stockman, yesterday had to admit that the worst dust storm he ever saw was on the Plains.

At the Panhandle-Plains Historical Society meeting in Canyon last week, Judge Hoover rather scoffed at the Panhandle dust storms. In fact he said the storm he was in the day after the territory of Oklahoma was opened to settlers, the famous Oklahoma Run, April 22, 1889, was worse than anything he had experienced in Texas.

But now Judge Hoover is in accord with the other Panhandle citizens in saying, "That storm Sunday—it was the worst I've ever seen."

FIVE

# NEWSPAPER REPORTS, LATER YEARS

Years after the Black Blizzard of April 14, 1935, the storm remains one of the central events of the Dust Bowl era in western Kansas, eastern Colorado, the Oklahoma and Texas panhandles, and eastern New Mexico. And much of the retelling about the storm has appeared in newspapers, books, and articles in both popular and scholarly publications. In the following accounts, some of the reminiscences will sound familiar. Also, there are newspaper stories that seem to relate to the big storm but have dated it differently. Many newspapers, especially those in areas in or near the Dust Bowl, printed extensive articles during the week of the fiftieth anniversary of the big storm in 1985. References in national publications were also frequent during that time. Some of the materials reprinted here are shortened, others are reprinted in their entirety to show the remarkable resilience of memories of the 1935 duster.

### Memory of Pampa's 1935 Duster Remains Sharp
By Wanda Huff
News Staff Writer
(The Pampa Daily News, *April 13, 1967*)

It's been 32 years since Pampa has been blacked out completely by a rolling, gritty dust storm like the "big one of '35," but Pampa residents have not forgotten.

They haven't forgotten the "whopping big blizzard" of '37 either, but as Mrs. Katie Vincent, resident here since 1903, said, "After those came in, I never worried any more. I just let them pass."

The dust storm of 1932 [*sic*] rolled in across the prairies without warning late one Sunday evening on April 14.

It disrupted church services, "messed up house cleaning" for months, and "scared some folks into thinking the world was coming to an end," Mrs. Vincent and Tracy Cary, founder of the Pampa Geneological [*sic*] and Historical Society, said.

The duster was described as ["]an ominous looking black cloud that boiled in from the northwest," and left behind tubfulls [*sic*] of dirt in every home in the city, Cary said.

"It was so bad we had to put wet cloths over our faces to breathe. I heard that people sitting in cars downtown couldn't see the outline of the person sitting next to them," Cary said. . . .

"That big one of 1935, some people were so scared they thought the world was coming to an end, because the sky turned to black. I couldn't even see the lights on our car. That's the worst storm I've ever seen in all my 60 years of living in the Panhandle," Mrs. Vincent said. . . .

*The following account of the March 3, 1935, black duster seems very familiar to those who were present to witness the Palm Sunday storm in April, except for the light rain shower.*

### BLACK SPRING: Beginning of the Dust Bowl
By George Turner
Globe-News Staff Writer
Sunday afternoon, March 3, 1935.
(Sunday News-Globe, *Amarillo, Texas, April 13, 1975*)

The towering black wall crouched on the western horizon, creeping steadily toward the city as a cat stalks a mouse. Everybody gaped in awe because neither we nor anybody else had ever seen anything like it.

"There's no telling what's in that!" my mother said as the rolling mass loomed ever larger. The thing resembled most a vast mass of smoke from a gigantic oil fire.

"It's almost here," my father said. "We'd better park the car." He curbed the Model A at a point on N. Fillmore near N.E. 6th. From the back seat I watched with fascination as the blackness crawled along, seemingly devouring the S & M Drug Store, Dreamland Cottage Camp, the Ferdinand Hotel and other then-familiar landmarks. Just as it reached us I looked at my dollar watch. It was 3:41.

The other cars were stopping now, some at the curb and a few in the traffic lanes. An elderly couple in a neighboring auto prayed earnestly. For a brief moment we were engulfed by a brown-grey cloud of dust that veiled but did not obscure the sun. Everybody's headlights lighted up.

Then the sun was blotted out and the darkness fell.

It was an unbelievable darkness, much blacker than mere night. My father turned on the dome light, but it faded into black. The headlights of all the other cars seemed to have been swallowed up. No light would penetrate the dark. We seemed to be smothering in dust.

Time passes slowly when you're frightened and choking in total darkness. It seemed a long time before the sun gradually returned the world to us. It was a beautiful climax worthy of Cecil B. DeMille: the light filtered through the waning dust in streaks of color, then a light rain shower fell and within minutes rainbows appeared. A critic would have said it was too dramatic.

Everybody was amazed to learn that the blackout lasted only about five minutes. It covered an area from Eastern New Mexico to Waynoka, Okla., from below Lubbock into the Oklahoma Panhandle. It seemed an amazing phenomenon and it was an historic one—the first black duster in history. We didn't realize that we hadn't seen the feature, just a preview of coming attractions.

It was difficult to believe that this thing was only a dust storm. We'd had many dusters during the past four years because of a prolonged drouth that dried the plowed fields and allowed winds to pick up the pulverized soil from open furrows. This storm was called a "freak of nature" by the U.S. Weather Bureau, which blamed a "change of wind" for creating a unique storm that changed daylight to night.

It didn't remain unique. There were others just as bad—

DUST STORM APPROACHING SPEARMAN, TEXAS 1935

*Postcards of disasters were fairly common, at least until World War II changed the way we look at disasters. What these photos show is the Black Sunday storm approaching Stratford and Spearman, Texas, on April 14, 1935.*

black ones from Eastern New Mexico and Kansas, red ones from Oklahoma that made it appear as though the world were on fire, yellow-tan ones with biting sand instead of dust. The "shift of wind" occurred with monotonous regularity.

Gene Howe, editor of the *Amarillo Globe*, tried to bolster our sagging spirits through his column, The Tactless Texan. On March 5 he mentioned that he was feeling better than usual because he had taken in a great quantity of "Vitamin K" during the storms. This miracle ingredient, he declared, was contained in atomized form in dust storms and was the reason we Panhandle folk were so strong and healthy and had the top football team in the state.

"Old Tack" had ample opportunity to ingest great quantities of the wonderful vitamin during the next several years.

The March 3 storm was a piker compared to one that hit during the night of March 27 and kept the city in darkness until mid-morning. It was the fastest black duster on record, traversing the 85 miles from Dalhart to Amarillo in one hour. Visibility was kept at or near zero for nine hours.

Traditionally, the worst duster of all occurred on another Sunday—April 14, 1935. It was the 30th storm to hit town since the March 3 storm. It moved down from the north, a monstrous wall of black dust clouds topped by an eerie fringe of yellow. Moving along ahead of it were incredibly high, spiraling dust-devils.

It rolled from Boise City, Okla., to Amarillo—105 miles—in exactly 105 minutes, arriving here at 7:30 P.M. Much of Kansas, Oklahoma, Colorado and New Mexico were blacked out by this monster, which dissipated at last in South Texas. It had been a beautiful day and thousands of Sunday drivers and picknickers were stranded on country roads and highways. Numerous children were missing, but all were found safe, eventually. On Wednesday the air was still filled with dust, sifting down from high altitudes long after the storm itself had passed.

Famed aviatrix Laura Ingalls, attempting to set a new non-stop transcontinental flying record in her new Lockheed low-wing monoplane, ran into the storm near Amarillo. She climbed to 23,000 feet but could not get above the clouds of dust. "It was the most appalling thing I ever saw in all my years of flying," Miss Ingalls said after making a forced landing at Alamosa, Colo.

Another pilot was seriously injured when the storm forced his plane down near Hutchinson, Kan., then flipped it over after he landed. A barnstorming parachutist was about to do his specialty over Dallas when the duster forced him to land. Massed prayers for rain were blacked out in Liberal and Guymon.

The dust lingered here for days, soon to be replaced by other storms and more dust. The Weather Bureau reported the cause of the April 14 debacle as a high pressure area which moved from the Dakotas to Wyoming, setting in motion a turbulence that headed south carrying topsoil from farms in Western Kansas and Oklahoma. . . .

### From the Sideline with Harold Hudson
### We Remember
### The Dust Bowl
(The Perryton (Texas) Herald, *May 12, 1983)*

[*After some remarks about a talk he gave to elementary school students about the Dust Bowl in general, Mr. Hudson continued his column with these reminiscences of the great black duster.*]
. . . The most famous dust storm that visited the Plains area came on a Sunday afternoon, April 14, 1935. We have a picture of this famous photograph of the dust cloud rolling over the houses of Perryton made by Perryton photographer W.E. Perry who had the presence of mind to get out his camera and photograph this historic event that day. It was a beautiful day in the Perryton area that Sunday afternoon, a really nice spring day, warm and with no wind. People were out riding around, picnicking on Wold Creek or Jines Springs, attending the Sunday matinee at the Ellis Theatre, maybe doing some yard work. Along in the middle of the afternoon, people began to see a huge dark cloud on the north horizon and it came closer.

As it came closer, you could see boiling clouds of dust, angry clouds highlighted by the sunshine glinting on the particles, and it was a frightening sight. Most people had never seen a dust storm like this one even though they had seen plenty of dusters. It was a time for flight and those who saw the approaching cloud in time headed for shelter. The dust storm is etched permanently in the memory of everyone who went through it, just as the memory of Pearl Harbor on another fateful Sunday afternoon is etched into the memory of those who experienced that historic event.

We remember that afternoon well. We had gone to Jines Springs, the favorite swimming spot about 10 miles south of town, just east of the former golf course. Our companions were Dean Blank, Edwin Orr and Tom Patton and we were young boys out for an afternoon of fun. Jines Springs is located below the caprock of the Wolf Creek valley and so it happened that nobody saw the approaching duster until it was actually pretty close. When we did notice this thing on the north horizon, we four climbed out of the pool, quickly dressed and headed for the highway to try to get back to town. We did catch a ride and made it as far as the top of the hill south of the cemetery when the angry cloud of dust rolled over us. It immediately turned pitch black. You couldn't see your hand in front of your face. We were petrified with fright, expecting the car to be hit by debris or swept into the air because we believed this to be a cyclone.

Instead, it was merely dust. But mighty heavy dust. We began to choke down on the stuff and someone remembered that we had wet bathing suits with us and we breathed through these, getting some relief. After a while we decided to move toward town. We took turns walking in front of the car's headlights, and actually felt our way because it was impossible to see the edge of the roadway. It took us six hours to make it into town and when we got out of the car a block from home we nearly panicked because we couldn't see any landmarks, no street signs or curbs or sidewalks. We more or less felt our way along, finally groping the distance to our home where we joined our nervous parents who didn't know where we were and had no way to get out and hunt for us.

We remember that the inside of our house was thick and hazy with the dust and it was dimly lit despite having all the lights turned on. Dust settled on everything. Although it did get somewhat lighter, this storm lasted all night long, and for the next two days before it finally cleared off. It was reported that this duster covered up the land all the way to the Gulf Coast and it was reported that ships 200 miles in the Atlantic Ocean were covered with dust swept that far out to sea by this monster. It was hard to calculate how many tons of topsoil moved through the air on that day.

We remember getting up in the morning and looking at the

white spot on our pillow where our head had been, the rest of the pillow brown with dust. Mother tried everything to keep out the dust. She used brown tape to seal the windows, hung wet sheets over windows and doors, still the dust came inside. Yet people survived these storms and while there were reports of "dust pneumonia" in this area, we never knew personally anybody who suffered from it. The human body is resilient and adapts to its environment. Or perhaps it took tough people to survive the dust storms of the 1930s. At any rate, the 1930 dust storms are like most harrowing experiences, better related afterwards than enjoyed during the performance.

*The following stories are reprinted from* The Tumbleweed Times *(Boise City, Oklahoma), October 1981, including the story about the Associated Press reporter who was caught by the storm on the way to Boise City. The first reprint here is about Robert Geiger's adventure on April 14, 1935.*

## BLACK SUNDAY—APRIL 14, 1935
### The Nation's Largest Black Duster

The Dust Bowl, KS, OK, NM, CO, TX (TNS)—During the 1930s the United States Weather Service didn't have its satellites up in the sky scanning the ground for signs of inclement weather. There was no sophisticated nerve center in Kansas City for forecasts. There were no teletypes and operators relaying instantaneous changes in the weather. In fact, there was no allied system of weather spotters on the ground pouring in information to any one source. There were local weather stations, to be sure, but the weather observers were measuring wind velocity and precipitation (when there was any) and recording it. Then they mailed in their reports to the weather bureau. The federal budget didn't allow for telephone calls, either.

The major wire services, Associated Press, United Press (later merged with International News Service to form UPI) and others didn't have as sophisticated a system of teletypes and photo wire services as they do today. Usually they were set up in the metropolitan areas, such as Denver, CO., with an office at one of the metro publications, just as AP was set up in the Denver Post

Building on April 14, 1935. Reporters for the wire service were assigned to a "beat" or region to cover. Back then there were not specialists or content editors, and writers such as there are now, but all-purpose reporters whose job it was to rush out in all kinds of weather, cover a story and either phone it back to the office from the spot—or if there were pictures, rush back to the office in a company car (or the reporter's own jalopy) and file the story.

The morning of April 14, 1935, seemed to Robert E. Geiger, AP reporter at the Denver office, to be just like any other, maybe a little better weatherwise. The birds were chirping and the sun was shining. Geiger and his counterpart, photographer H. G. Eisenhard, loaded down their car with flash bulbs, camera paraphernalia and other necessary odds and ends and proceeded along Highway 287. They were headed for Boise City, OK, and perhaps on to Guymon, OK. Geiger had been assigned the beat by AP and he knew where the heart of the dust bowl was—he had been in it many times, covering the storms and phoning his stories back to Denver.

They always got front page play in the *Denver Post,* not only because his stories were lucid and "colorful," but because Geiger was an excellent reporter, picking up little details and using them in their proportion, never overlooking anything that might be interesting if his story happened to be read in Peoria, Ill.

The National Weather Service, which was then referred to as "The Weather Bureau" by just about everybody, had received calls from the Bismarck, North Dakota, area early that morning that winds were picking up in velocity and that there was local swirling dust on the ground and in the air.

About 10 A.M., a front moved over the Dakotas and by noon winds were reported traveling at speeds up to 100 MPH in parts of Nebraska. Sometime between 12 noon and 1 P.M. a black duster formed along the Kansas-Nebraska line, between Denver and Southwestern Iowa—a black duster of monstrous proportions. Black Sunday was officially underway. The cyclonic winds hurled the Dakotas dust into Nebraska and finally Nebraska and Dakotas dust combined with Kansas dust to form a dust cloud—at its epicenter—of dynamic turbulence. The roller moved in a generally southerly direction, but to most residents seemed to be coming from the northeast. The winds were kicking up the dirt at the ground and hurling it 20,000 feet into the air, while at the same time the roller was churning dirt in a cylindrical fashion, in what local observers termed a "sidewinder," or "horizontal tornado."

What they were referring to was what weather experts today refer to as a "cyclogenic" storm system, common to Eastern Colorado or Southwestern Kansas, which gives the strongest winds for the longest period of time. Other dust storms of those days were generated by moving cold fronts, downslope winds from the Rockies, and thunderstorms. Some fronts produced just as intense rollers as that of April 14, 1935, even if they didn't cover the vast area that the 1935 roller covered. The vastness of the Black Sunday roller was reflected by the fact that dust black-outs were occurring over all of Kansas and Eastern Colorado, all of Oklahoma, Eastern New Mexico, Texas, Western Arkansas, Missouri, Nebraska, the Dakotas and the lower half of Iowa. All in all the roller was some 1,000 miles wide, traveling 1,500 miles south-southeast before it finally broke up and scattered into the Gulf of Mexico.

Geiger and Eisenhard were just ahead of the roller. Every now and then Geiger and Eisenhard would stop the car and get out. Eisenhard would take a shot of the roller with his camera. There was plenty of sunlight for available light as long as the two reporters stayed ahead of the roller. They moved in this fashion for over 200 miles, just ahead of the roller, driving through Campo, CO, crossing the state line into Oklahoma, across the Cimarron River bridge north of Boise City and through the hills south of the river to the Herman Schneider farm, just a short distance north of Boise City. There Geiger stopped the car, because he noted that a car was stranded in the bar ditch. It was full of people. They might need help.

While Geiger and Eisenhard were travelling south ahead of the roller, Moe Atkins, eight-year-old son of Mr. and Mrs. John Atkins of La Junta, CO, was playing with Keith and Kenneth Skelly and John Tuttle, 12-year-old boys, at the stockyards in South Boise City, OK.

The boys saw the roller coming Sunday afternoon at about 4 P.M. "It didn't scare us because we didn't have enough sense to be scared," Moe said. The roller appeared to be travelling at about 15 to 20 MPH, although the weather bureau estimated the winds overhead and behind the roller at 100 MPH. But it took the massive dust cloud about an hour to move 20 or 30 miles, according [to] the time estimated by residents of towns in an east-west line, such as Campo-Elkhart, Boise City-Guymon and Stratford-Dalhart-Texhoma. It was almost two hours from the time the duster rolled into Elkhart until it rolled into Keyes and Boise City. It was two hours later that it rolled into Dalhart, Stratford and Texhoma. For some reason the movement of the roller on the ground was not equivalent to the wind velocities on top of or behind the roller itself.

Mr. and Mrs. John Atkins decided that the cloud coming in would pass over and clear up, so they decided to take Moe and his sister, Mary Ruth, and return to La Junta. When the Atkins car reached the Herman Schneider farm, about five miles north of Boise City, the car ran off the road into the ditch along the highway and got stuck in the sand. Geiger and Eisenhard stopped and retrieved the Atkins family from their car. Eisenhard snapped a picture of the duster at the Schneider farm which was to become one of the most widely published roller pictures ever disseminated by the American press. It was run in the *Denver Post* the next day and fed out to other metro newspapers after it ran in the *Post*. Almost every big daily in the country picked up the picture, not because it was unique, but because it was the only picture available at the time it was received by each of the dailies through courier. Geiger and Eisenhard had taken the first available shots of the April 14, 1935 Black Sunday and by random selection some photo editor picked that one picture to run on the front page [*actually page 3*] of the *Post* with accompanying cutline written by Geiger, who could always think of catch phrases at the right time for the right occasion. Geiger and Eisenhard had beaten every reporter in the country with pictures on Black Sunday because Geiger had the hunches and Eisenhard had the camera ready.

When Geiger and Eisenhard made it to Boise City and unloaded the Atkins family, they raced over to the Boise City News and got prints made of their negatives. Then their car wouldn't start. The ignition was victim to a common ailment during those days. Static electricity had rendered it useless, at least for the time being.

Geiger offered $50 to anyone in Boise City who would take

him to Denver and guarantee to get him there in time to run the picture in the next day's edition of the *Denver Post*. Asa Pitzer, who felt like he could use the money in those hard times, volunteered and fought the dust storm all the way into Denver that night. Pitzer's driving and Geiger's tenacity got himself and Eisenhard a scoop.

But Geiger's fame was not for getting this picture and story of the Black Sunday storm in print. It was for inventing the term "dust bowl." On another occasion during the 30s when Geiger was on one of his forays for dust storm stories, he called in a story by phone from Guymon, OK. In his lead paragraph he used "Three little words . . . if it rains." In between these six little words he inserted "dust bowl," never knowing that his catchy beginning and end words would be overlooked in favor of the phrase "dust bowl." It caught the public imagination as representative of a part of the nation during a period of time when nothing seemed to be going right. It has been used since then all over the world to represent the part of the world and the period of time represented. . . .

*Though much of the following article repeats what has been said before, some details about the origins of the storm did not appear in other sources. Bensch's description of the big storm's meteorological origins are the most specific encountered in research for this publication, especially the discussion of the cold front that was barely mentioned in any of the interviews or in the newspaper accounts of the storm. The editor's note below is the newspaper's note.*

### April 14, 1935: Total, overwhelming darkness
By Randall Bensch

(Dodge City Daily Globe, *April 13, 1985;*
The Southwest Daily Times, *Liberal, Kansas, April 14, 1985*)

*Ed. note: About the author: Randall Bensch grew to manhood in the Oklahoma Panhandle, which has been a part of the 1930's dust bowl. He holds the BS in Physics from Oklahoma State University and the MS in Meteorology from the University of Oklahoma. Bensch has taught meteorology in Louisiana and Oklahoma. He now resides on a farm near his childhood home of Logan, Ok., where he is actively involved in farm-*

*ing and dairying. Since early 1984 he has been the staff meteorologist for*
*K-101 (KWOX) FM radio of Woodward, Ok.*

Black Sunday, April 14, 1935, brought the single most dramatic dust storm of the whole dust bowl era. The storm was not as widespread as several of the others that occurred during those years. The severe dustiness was confined to the southern Great Plains. But where it occurred, it was, without doubt, the most overwhelming of all dust storms. Those who went through it have never forgotten the experience.

During the mid-1930's, there were many dust storms both major and minor. Sometimes the dust was confined to a small local area and at other times large clouds of dust were swept high into the atmosphere and carried hundreds or even thousands of miles.

The first major dust storm that received national attention occurred Nov. 12-13, 1933. It originated mainly in the northern plains, in Nebraska and the Dakotas, and the dust was carried eastward all the way to the Atlantic. Another such widespread dust storm came during the period May 9–12, 1934. These early dust storms were more severe in the northern states than elsewhere.

But, in 1935 the center of dust activity shifted southward into eastern Colorado, eastern New Mexico, western Kansas, western Oklahoma and the Texas and Oklahoma panhandles. There were numberous [sic] dusty days in February, March and early April of that year, but the big storm, the one more remembered than any other, came on April 14.

Joe L. Todd, oral historian with the Oklahoma Historical Society, has called the Black Sunday storm "the worst dust storm of the 1930s. There were other dust storms that lasted longer. There were other storms with stronger winds. But this one produced total darkness."

Under clear warm skies a towering wall of dust marched southward. The churning dust cloud could be seen coming for several miles.

Rudolph Trieber of Shattuck, Ok., recalls, "It came from the north, boiling, with birds flying ahead of it." After the storm arrived, "for a few minutes there was total darkness. You couldn't see your hand in front of your face."

Just what produced this dramatic dust storm? What combination of weather features and other factors came together to produce such an awesome natural event?

Obviously, the first thing that was needed for a dust storm of this magnitude was much loose powdery soil. Drought during the months and years preceding April 1935, had prevented the normal growth of crops and pastures. The wheat crop planted during the fall of 1934 had suffered from dry windy weather and provided little ground cover during the spring of 1935. The months of February and March brought frequent spells of strong winds, which further stirred up the soil and destroyed much of the remaining wheat cover.

The early days of April were also quite windy. An intense low pressure storm center passed through northern Kansas on the 10th and brought strong northerly winds across the high plains. At Dodge City this storm was described as the worst up to that time in terms of duration and visibility. Semidarkness prevailed during most of the daylight hours on the 10th and 11th.

But high pressure then settled into the region on the 12th and brought a spell of clear warming spring weather.

The day now known as Black Sunday was actually, for the most part, a warm sunny day. In fact, over the entire region it was the warmest day of the month with highs well up into the 80s and even above 90 degrees some places. In Kansas, Dodge City hit 84 and Wichita 83, Oklahoma City reached 86 and Amarillo 90. Farther south, Abilene, Tx., reached a hot 96-degree reading.

But, even as calm sunny weather was spreading across the southern Great Plains, conditions were developing to the north that would soon bring an abrupt end to the peaceful springtime scene.

The Black Sunday storm had its origin as a cold Canadian polar air mass that first appeared in the Yukon Territory on April 12. The leading edge of the polar air was a strong cold front that advanced into Montana on the 13th accompanied by gale force winds and rapidly falling temperatures. Heavy wet snow produced blizzard con[di]tions in central Montana on the 13th.

As the cold front moved southward through the plains, it left the precipitation behind. It was now a dry front but still strong with a sharp temperature contrast, the kind of front that is often referered [sic] to as a "norther." As the much cooler air met the warmer air, a strong density difference was produced.

This helped drive the winds. The heavier cool air rushed southward to replace the warm air in its path.

The cool air moving over the sun-warmed ground caused great instability. Heating from below produced rising air currents and boiling churning action immediately behind the advancing cold front.

Similar situations are occasionally produced on a much smaller scale by summer thunderstorms. Cool outrushing air from a thunderstorm meets the surrounding hot air and there is tremendous rising motion. Where there is bare ground, such as in the deserts, a local dust storm called a "haboob" is produced. These are fairly common in the southern Sahara and not unusual in the southwestern deserts of the United States.

But the Black Sunday storm, caused by a major cold front passing over the powdery-fine soils of the nation's heartland, was much more widespread and dense than desert storms produced over rocky or sandy surfaces.

By early afternoon on the 14th, the strong cold front had reached the dry soils of drought-stricken western Kansas and eastern Colorado. Great clouds of dust were swept up in the boiling churning winds. Soon, the dust cloud had darkened, outlining the advancing cold front.

At 2:40 P.M. the storm swept into Dodge City. Quickly the city was overwhelmed in chilling darkness and choking dust.

Advancing southward at a speed of about 40 miles per hour, the dust-bearing cold front reached northwest Oklahoma by 4 P.M. It then advanced into the Texas Panhandle.

The weather observed at Canadian, Tx., near the point of the dust storm's greatest severity, reported the following conditions. At 4:52 P.M. skies were essentially clear with just a few high thin clouds, visibility was seven miles, winds were a gentle 8 MPH from the northeast and the temperature was a very warm 87 degrees F.

Then at 5:47 P.M. the dust storm hit. Only five minutes later at 5:52 P.M. the temperature had drop[p]ed to 61 degrees, winds were howling from the northeast at 50 MPH, with stronger gusts, and visibility was zero. By 11 P.M. the winds had diminished to 30 MPH and the moon was dimly visible.

The dust cloud reached Oklahoma City at 6:35 P.M. and Amarillo at 7:15 P.M. All along the way, visibilities dropped to zero.

During the nighttime hours, winds diminished as the cold front slowly weakened.

The dust mass moved primarily into New Mexico and far west Texas early on Monday April 15. Visibility dropped to zero at Wink and Guadalupe Pass in Texas and down to one-eighth mile at Albuquerque and Roswell in New Mexico. Most of central and southeast Texas escaped the dust. Visibility [w]as never lower than six miles at Dallas and five miles at San Antonio. Houston missed the dust completely.

To those who went through the Black Sunday storm, the experience was unforgettable. The hours immediately preceding the storm's arrival provided an opportunity to enjoy a balmy spring day. After the dusty weather of the previous week, many people spent time outdoors in the warm sunshine.

Then along the horizon to the north a dark cloud appeared. At first it looked somewhat like an ordinary cloud, perhaps even a rain cloud. But, as it approached it took on a more ominous appearance. Moving silently southward it presented itself as a boiling churning wall of dust that extended from the ground upward for several hundred feet. Upon its arrival, almost total darkness was produced along with strong north to northeast winds and falling temperatures. Even with artificial lighting, it was possible to see only a very short distance. The dust was overpowering and choking, making it difficult to breathe.

"Unbelievable" is the way Rudolph Treiber describes it. "You'd've had to see it and experience it to believe anything like this could happen."

Other dust storms followed, but none were ever as overwhelming as the Black Sunday storm.

### Worst Storm Hit on Black Sunday
By Sandy Bryant
(Dodge City Daily Globe, *April 13, 1985;*
The Southwest Daily Times, *Liberal, Kansas, April 14, 1985)*

Sunday marks the 50th anniversary of what most people call the worst dust storm to ever hit this area—Black Sunday.

When the rolling dust cloud struck Dodge City on April 14, 1935, the intensity of the storm caught many people by surprise and stories from the *Dodge City Daily Globe* on April 15 give accounts of numerous children and even adults being lost in the dark cloud.

"A party of eight junior high school boys and girls marooned for 12 hours in the dust storm, Sunday afternoon, another of five boys of the same age until Monday, and dozens of small children separated from their parents for an hour or more at the beginning of the storm were the results of a dust cloud that swooped down from the northeast at 3 o'clock Sunday afternoon with the blackness of midnight," the *Globe* reported.

The articles gave accounts of men at the golf course having to crawl to find their way to the club house to get out of the storm and another man getting out of his car because he was unable to see to drive, crawling toward his home and arriving at the house of a neighbor.

Records from the National Weather Service office at the Dodge City Municipal Airport show that the sun rose on a clear day at 6:06 A.M. with the wind from the west. By 7 A.M. the wind had shifted to the northwest.

The temperature for the day peaked at 84 degrees at 2 P.M. and by 3 P.M. the temperature had fallen to 80 degrees. During the next hour, the temperature dropped 18 degrees to 62 degrees. By 5 P.M. the thermometer showed a reading of 53 degrees.

Winds shifted to due north between 11 A.M. and 5 P.M. and speeds peaked between 2 P.M. and 7 P.M., when the northerly winds were clocked at more than 30 miles per hour.

Alonzo A. Justice, the supervisor of the weather bureau from 1919 through 1936, included a detailed description of the storm in his record of the day.

He wrote, "Dust continued from the 13th with visibility around one mile (illegible word) and up to 9 or 10 A.M. when objects three or four miles away could be seen.

"At 2:40 (P.M.) sharp a great, black dust cloud came down from the north. It was estimated at 500 or 600 feet in height and came at a rate of 50 or 60 miles per hour.

"The instant it struck, almost total darkness set in. It certainly was as dark as midnight for about 40 minutes, after which there were occasional slight breaks.

"Visibility not more than 10 feet at lowest.

"The onrushing cloud, the darkness and the thick, choking

dirt make this storm one of terror and the worst, while it lasted, ever known here.

"Many people were caught out and several cases are related of children being lost, though rescued later.

"By midnight, the visibility had risen above 1,000 feet. The danger to soil blowing was not as serious as the one on the 10–11.

"One Dodge City businessman, caught in a half block of home tried to crawl home but wound up a half block away at the home of friends.

"It is said by observers that hundreds of birds, geese, ducks and other kinds (of birds), were seen flying in front of the dust cloud. A number of dead small birds were seen on the ground after the storm."

The first recorded rain following the dust storm was on April 17, when a light mist fell on Dodge City.

### Black Sunday: No One Who Was Here Can Forget 50 Years Ago Today
By Esther Groves
Times Area Editor
(The Southwest Daily Times, *Liberal, Kansas, April 14, 1985*)

No one who experienced Black Sunday here exactly 50 years ago on April 14, 1935, has forgotten that day.

Alf Landon was Kansas governor. The Dustbowl years had already begun in fields around Liberal, "there were blowouts all over—blown out down to the hardpan," recalled Charles Brisendine, 804 Elm.

"Schools dismissed for dust storms," George Mead, 115 S. Calhoun, said, "and we found our way home by the curbs. Once a couple of children got lost going home from McDermott School in a dust storm and they found them in the north part of town."

The strange thing about April 14 was that it started out as "a beautiful day—clear blue skies," Brisendine said. "I was thirteen and out hunting arrowheads east of town."

He had barely walked home to 815 New York when "we noticed this cloud on the horizon. It came up very rapidly, looking like a huge drapery with folds and convolutions in it. It was fascinating but scary."

What seemed odd to George Mead was that "the sun was shining, and yet this black cloud was coming closer—it was weird."

According to *The Southwest Tribune,* the Liberal newspaper of that time:

"A rolling cloud of dust several thousand feet high, moving at about 35 miles an hour, arrived from the north at 3:50 o'clock Sunday afternoon (and) enveloped the city and the county. . . . Those who saw the approaching cloud stated that the high mass appeared to roll; that there were flocks of birds flying a short distance ahead of the dust, trying to keep away from the storm. The day had been clear and warm, and many people were out driving."

What happened to some of those Sunday drivers is remembered by Bill Hirn, 839 S. Washington, because he was at a filling station at the junction of U.S. 83 and 54 when the storm hit:

"It got so dark you couldn't see the pumps out front of the station. You could just barely see the light in the ceiling. . . .

"There was a bunch of people at the Country Club. They tried to go west on 54 but their cars wouldn't go right, either because of static electricity or too much dirt in the air. Some went off into the barditch. They walked back to the filling station. Their faces were dirty but when they took their hats off, their heads were as shiny as a new dollar!"

Everett Mead, 706 S. Jordan, father of George Mead, "was just coming in from fishing. I drove up in the yard and it hit. By the time I stopped the car and got out I couldn't even see the house."

He got to the house only to find his wife and children weren't there. "I went to the storm cave and it was full—my family and Aleen and Alvin House . . . (so) full, in fact, I didn't get quite down the steps." They stayed there until everything was over.

Everett Higgins, 19 S. Prospect, was "on the farm out by Hayne [when?] it came. . . . I was out breaking some colts and had two tied to a wagon. I told my father-in-law, 'We better get those colts in the barn.'"

But when they walked out of the barn, "there was a big black cloud . . . so dark we couldn't see the house 200 yards away. My wife lit a mantle kerosene lamp and set it on a chair at the east window. I couldn't see where I was going but was feeling my way with my hand out. I couldn't see the light until I touched the window with my hand. . . .

"Two boys were playing baseball at Hayne. They ran for the barpit—the ditch along 54—and lay down in that until it was over."

Ed Hardey, 1007 N. Lincoln, "was in Hugoton, and a ball game was going on at the ball ground at Hugoton High School. At first no one was worried about (the black cloud)."

Hardey had to go to work, so he took off, headed to town and got his lunch—and the storm hit. "It was total darkness. I couldn't drive. I couldn't go to work. I pulled over to the curb and parked until it was over.

"Eighteen people in Hugoton died from dust pneumonia that year. They used the Methodist Church basement for a hospital in those days because there was no hospital."

"We'd carry tubs full of water," Higgins said, "and wring (sheets) out and hang 'em at the windows to filter out dust. You could wake up in the morning and write your name anywhere."

In Liberal, Brisentine said, "We just stood and watched it come up. I think we expected to be blown away when it hit. As I recall, we came inside just before the dirt hit, and everything turned black outside. . . . It grew dark in the house, we had to turn on the lights, and there were haloes around all the lights."

Mead remembered that "you could put your hand up right in front of your nose and not see it."

*The Southwest Tribune* said those who had not noticed the approaching black cloud "were somewhat astonished to see the sun suddenly disappear."

Among the astonished were those attending funeral services for Lee Wilson at First United [*sic*] Methodist Church. "It got the darkest dark you ever saw," said Mary Brewington, 619 E. Second. "Some stayed at church but I walked home . . . . I just walked down the street and didn't turn right or left.

"When I got home, there was a strange horse that had drifted into the old garage by the house while I was at the funeral."

The newspaper reported that "the dust deposit extended from the foothills of the Rocky Mountains to the Mississippi River."

The same issue announced that a buffalo barbecue scheduled in Liberal for the Thursday after Black Sunday would be canceled because merchants didn't want to chance barbecuing meat in a sandstorm.

*Articles from a special edition of the* Guymon (Oklahoma) Daily Herald *(April 13–14, 1985), like those in other papers published to commemorate the Palm Sunday black duster, talk about other storms and the Dust Bowl in general, but they are reprinted in full because they reflect the general feeling of the time as well as that in regard to the big storm itself.*

## Black Sunday . . .
## Area Residents Remember Events on 50th Anniversary
By Maurine Dunkerson
Managing Editor
(Guymon (Oklahoma) Daily Herald, *April 13–14, 1985*)

It was 50 years ago, Sunday, April 14, 1935. The day dawned clear, warm and sunny. Little did Panhandle residents realize before the day was over they would be bowled over by a dust storm so black they could not see their hands in front of their faces.

This Sunday went down in the annals of history as the grand[d]addy of all dust storms. Some say "Black Sunday" climaxed the dust storms and the intensity lessened after that date. Some say the dusters came with more regularity after that Sunday. Dusters were still reported until after 1937.

"We had dusters for about two years," said Burnell Focks, "before this one hit. It was the worst we had but it seemed like they weren't quite so bad after that."

Focks said he and his buddies were swimming in one of their "swimming holes" when they saw the dust rolling in on the horizon. It was quite a ways away so like most kids they kept on swimming. When it began to get a little closer, they decided they'd better scatter for their homes.

Focks walked a quarter of a mile, to where the cows were in the pasture, to get them home before the storm struck. However, it was too late and the dust clouds hit just as he got there.

He had his dog with him and he could hear him barking but couldn't see him. He immediately dropped to the ground

IN HANDIE DUST STORM APPROACHING - APRIL 14, 1935
NO. 4    THE PERRY STUDIO - PERRYTON, TEXAS.

*Postcards showing Black Sunday storm approaching Perryton, Texas, April 14, 1935.*

HANDIE DUST STORM APPROACHING
APRIL 14, 1935    THE PERRY STUDIO
PERRYTON, TEXAS.

and crawled to the fence line. From there he made his way to the gate, across the road and into the pasture by his house.

Another resident who was a small child on Black Sunday, Neta Jones, said since it was a nice day, the family was out riding. Her father saw the cloud and hurriedly drove back home. He told everyone to get into the storm shelter while he put the car in the garage and shut the door.

"When we came out of the storm cellar," said Mrs. Jones, "the car was sitting out but the garage door was shut. My father got so excited about getting everything shut down, he forgot to put the car in the garage."

"We thought it was the end of time," another elderly resident said. "We all rushed to the storm cellar and even though it wasn't the end of the world, it was still stuffy."

"You could always tell if you slept peacefully during the dust bowl days," said Focks. "If the pillow had an outline of your head you slept peaceful but if it was dirty all over you were restless."

Jeanette Knowles from Texhoma recalls April 14, 1935. "Our first sight of the strange looking bank showing up in the northeast had an eerie appearance even then. Then as it grew and grew we became more and more uneasy, not knowing just what was behind the ominous looking cloud," she explained.

She was living at home with her parents, Albert and Cora Wilson. They all congregated in the central room of their home. The room had an east window onto a porch.

Her father was a photographer and always had a camera at hand so he made preparations to snap some pictures of the on-coming storm. When the full force of the storm struck Texhoma she said it was complete and total darkness.

"We could no longer even see that there was a window on the east side of that room," Mrs. Knowles recalled.

"From then on, these dust storms became a regular thing. Cleaning up from them was not easy. The dust that settled over everything in the house was of a powdery consistency that just would not wipe off," she continued.

Like everyone else in the Panhandle during those dust storm days, they tried to make the house more dust-proof by sealing all the windows and frames around the windows and doors with masking tape and sometimes hung wet sheets over windows to trap some of the dust.

Mrs. Knowles' brother, Erwin Wilson, was attending college at Goodwell and driving back and forth from Texhoma. Many times on the trip home he would drive right into the southwest wind. The grit pitted the windshield and blasted the paint off the front of the car.

Many people kept wet sheets and towels hung over their doors and windows in those days. In fact, sometimes when they saw the dust rolling in it was the first thing they would do. It was too hard to breathe otherwise.

Richard Reeder also remembers "Black Sunday." He said he was outside playing when the neighbors noticed the black duster rolling toward Guymon. Everyone took shelter in their houses and began putting sheets and towels over the windows. As the storm got worse they began to wet them so they could breathe.

When the storm had abated a little, Reeder had to go milk the cow. There was only one problem. That night they had chocolate milk—or at least it was the color of chocolate milk.

"There was one good thing that came from the dust," Reeder said laughingly. "The houses were better insulated because of all the dust collecting in the attics."

## Black Sunday: 50 Years Ago, Dust Storm Raked Panhandle
### By Gil Broyles
### (Associated Press Writer)
### (The Champaign-Urbana (Illinois) News-Gazette, *April 14, 1985*)

GUYMON, Okla.—Rain comes grudgingly to the Oklahoma Panhandle, where farmers of the 1980s coax startling grain and livestock production from the dry land.

But nature had the upper hand 50 years ago when Guymon was at the hub of a historical disaster that gave its name to a region and a decade—the Dust Bowl.

Among the hundreds of dust storms that raked western Oklahoma and parts of Kansas, Colorado, New Mexico and Texas from 1933 to 1937, one stands out to those who stayed with their beloved land.

April 14, 1935, dawned as a warm, clear Palm Sunday. It became instead the day of the Black Blizzard—Black Sunday.

"It was intense darkness. As dark as could be," said Laurence Drake, 78, who was caught in the middle of an alfalfa field. "It scared us. We didn't know what was going to happen next."

The storm threw the farmers' naive abuse of the fragile plains back into their faces.

"It definitely woke a lot of people up that we were misusing the land," said Drake, who has spent a lifetime farming the Panhandle and working for soil and water conservation.

Settlers who squatted in the Panhandle before the turn of the century, when it was known as "No Man's Land," were joined by thousands more before Oklahoma became a state in 1907. Over the decades, they plowed up the soil's protective grass and, when the rains stopped, the wind began to lift the fine dirt.

"The one-way plow was the worst thing we could do," Drake said.

By 1935, dust storms had become a familiar and costly inconvenience for farmers and ranchers. The Oklahoma Panhandle, a row of three block-shaped counties with an area about that of Connecticut, was rattled by a dust storm on average every five days in the worst of the "dirty '30s."

But April 1935 was the cruelest month in a region that averaged 19 inches of rain a year, little or no rain fell that month. The Panhandle reported heavy to moderate dust on 20 of 30 days, according to the U.S. Department of Agriculture weather bureau.

In the week before April 14, blinding dust forced schools to close. A southeastern Colorado store ran out of sponges, which people used as dust masks. It took a 100-man search party to find two Vanceville, Kan., youngsters who lost their way in the swirling dust on a hunt for Indian arrowheads.

On April 10, according to newspaper accounts, 36 truckloads of furniture were counted moving furniture west out of Guymon.

Some were farmers giving up on the land, identified in the parlance of the day as "exodusters." Most were migrants passing through the devastated Dust Bowl on their way to California.

The term "Okie" eventually was applied to all displaced people making their way west.

The aging jalopy burdened with possessions became an icon of the era, an image burned into the national consciousness by thousands of pictures made by federal photographers, by John Steinbeck's 1939 novel, "The Grapes of Wrath," and by the movie, starring Henry Fonda, a year later.

On Thursday, April 11, a minor league baseball game in Oklahoma City was suspended because of heavy dust. On Friday and Saturday the dust began to clear. By Sunday, Oklahomans were looking forward to a clear day and a break from the dust.

It was Laurence Drake's 28th birthday. He and a helper were taking advantage of the good weather to work an irrigation canal running from the Cimarron River to a "little patch of alfalfa" on land his family had settled 50 years before.

"I looked up and noticed this terrible black cloud in the northwest," said Drake, who still farms near Gate, where the Panhandle is attached to the rest of the state.

"About half the sky, I guess," he recalled. "It looked like a terrible rainstorm."

Racing an estimated 40 MPH ahead of a cold front pressing down from Colorado and Kansas, the storm was upon the men in seconds. The darkness was complete except for static electricity arcing eerily within the roiling dust.

Through the blackness, Drake shouted to his co-worker. Using their shovels as blind men use white canes, they edged along the canal. When they were within arm's reach, the intense darkness still kept them invisible to each other.

Elsewhere, motorists out for Sunday drives had to halt their Model Ts in the middle of roads. Farmers fell to their knees and crawled to their houses. Their wives stretched dampened sheets across windows in a futile attempt to keep out the choking dust.

Families lit kerosene lanterns against the entombing darkness and waited.

"It was just like night. It just sifted in, no matter how good your house was, the dust was so fine." said Drake's wife, Winona.

Thousands of feet high and extending beyond the 168-mile length of the Panhandle, the storm took only minutes to sweep out of Kansas, cross the 34-mile-wide strip and boil southward into the Texas Panhandle like a moving mountain range.

For 10 to 15 minutes, no light penetrated the silt-like dirt. Later, the pall of heavy dust left behind muffled sound and made outdoor activities nearly impossible.

And those who had gathered three times daily in a Guymon church to pray for rain knew their prayers would go unanswered a while longer.

The dust from this and other storms drifted into dunes along fence rows and outbuildings. Planting became impossible, wheat was barely in the ground before the wind would dig it up.

The federal Resettlement Administration, predecessor of the Farm Home Administration, set up a program to provide small grants, about $10 to $30 a month, to the destitute.

Drake administered the program in Beaver County from 1935 to 1937, evaluating requests for help.

"Our office was filled every day almost. . . . It was unbelievable," Drake said. "There were very, very poor conditions. They were existing almost. They kept thinking that things would get better.

"It was just survival. Some of them had to leave. They just give up."

From 1930 to 1940, the population of the three Panhandle counties dropped from 30,960 to 21,198. Nearly one in three succumbed to the vise grip of dust and Depression.

But the survivors learned new ways of treating the land. Under President Franklin Roosevelt's New Deal, the U.S. Forest Service planted millions of acres of trees and shrubs on farms to serve as shelter-belts and reduce wind erosion.

The U.S. Department of Agriculture Soil Conservation Service began digging the first of more than 2000 small lakes in Oklahoma to control flooding and provide irrigation.

But rising prices for the fuel that powers irrigation pumps, a receding underground water supply and low farm prices raise the spectre of new dust storms.

[*The same article appeared in* The Pampa News *on April 14, 1985, with the addition of three paragraphs not included at the end of the above article.*]

Now, in a state which ranks among the top five in wheat and hay production, the Panhandle counties are among the most prolific producers. Some of the largest cattle feedlot operations in the world dot the Panhandle, accounting for a thick slice of the state's beef production. . . . But rising prices . . .

"The poorest conservation measure for farmers is low farm prices," said U.S. Rep. Glenn English, D-Okla., whose district includes much of western Oklahoma. "Like every small businessman during tough economic times, the farmer must squeeze every dollar out of his assets.

"That land is once again being plowed up. It's highly erodable land. Shelter belts that have been there since the time of the Great Depression are being torn out.

"Conservation is deteriorating, erosion of the land is increasing. If we find ourselves in a dry period of time for two or three years, we could see the dirt blow."

# SIX
# MISCELLANEOUS RESPONSES

Besides eyewitness and newspaper accounts of the great Black Blizzard, there is quite a variety of responses to the event. What follows are bits of humor, some doggerel verse, ballads, a one-act play, and articles about peripheral matters concerning dust in general during the 1930s.

## Humor Found Even in Black Blizzard Incidents
### By Frank Stallings
(Guymon Daily Herald—Pioneer Edition,
*Saturday–Sunday, April 13–14, 1985*)

Even in the worst of times, people in the Dust Bowl maintained some of their sanity by making light of conditions they had no power to change. It is not surprising that during the great Black Blizzard of 1935 incidents real and imagined caused smiles or even laughter.

These people laughed, bitterly perhaps, because nature had played a trick on them on April 14, only two weeks after she had patted them with a terrible April Fool's Day joke of another memorable duster. What rolled out of the north that Palm Sunday was not a prairie fire as some thought. Nor was it a "sideways tornado" as someone else first believed. But the worst joke was that it was not a rain cloud, and those who ran for storm cellars often were forced back into their houses by the suffocating dust that sifted into those

133

cellars. One woman remembers her mother looking at the rolling dust and remarking, "Isn't that the funniest looking thing?" Funny, indeed! If nature's joke was not funny, some non-human antics were. Farm families reported chickens roosting where they were when dust turned mid-afternoon into midnight. Those poor chickens must have thought it was a very short day. It seems miraculous that no one mentioned losing any chickens in that stifling dust.

One family's mule that habitually brayed every day at noon but at no other time broke his usual silence on that evening with "the loudest bray I ever heard in my life, like a cry of anguish that he was left out [of doors]. It was some unnatural phenomenon."

One woman struggled home through the darkness of the storm to discover that her yellow angora cat had climbed the brick wall of her house and was clinging to the screen over the kitchen window. The cat was not yellow when it was rescued.

Some animals did suffer. An English bulldog, which has a face that looks like it needs help anyway, required constant attention (wet towels held to his nose) during the big duster because he couldn't breathe in the dust. The process was made even more complicated because taking the dog outdoors to the bathroom required two persons—one to hold the dog's leash and the other to hold the wet towel over his nose.

So many people were outdoors on that bright and sunny day that it is no wonder hundreds were caught in their cars or even working. One farmer out in a field running a lister (to form ditches intended to combat the blowing away of his land) saw the ominous black cloud and continued working, thinking, "Well, I can make one more round. I didn't. I knew it was coming, but I didn't know it was coming that fast."

Seeing that the closed windows and doors were not keeping out the dust, one practical woman finally suggested that maybe if they would open the front door and the back door the dust would just blow on through. Another woman put it this way: "We got a lot of somebody's dirt that day."

A rancher said, "I had a neighbor who was bringing in a load of cattle at the time (the storm hit). This guy cussed every breath. When this cloud came in he quit cussin' right then."

A toper out for a drive in a Model A Ford told of putting the windshield down [*they could at that time be folded down to lie on the hood*] to get the breeze in his face. "I had been nipping more than a little that day. I went out to meet it and nearly choked to death before I got back to town."

Many others had what might be called religious experiences because of the Black Blizzard [*several remember hearing it called the Black Buzzard*]. Many people thought the storm was bringing the end of the world.

But not everyone. One man trying to ease his wife's terror told her it couldn't be the end of the world because the Bible didn't say the world was going to end that way. During a Sunday afternoon church service, someone rushed in to report the approach of the black monster. Someone else asked if this was the cloud mentioned in Revelation 1:7 that was to bring the Lord back. No, the preacher said, it would be "mighty queer for the Lord to come back in a cloud—of dust."

The looks of the storm brought out some apt questions and answers from children such as the boy who, looking at the rolling monster, asked his father, "Daddy, do you know how to pray?"

A little girl was reported to have looked out the window at the rolling dust and said, "Oh, look here, God's coming!" The distraught parent replied, "It looks more like hell to me."

Another parent told his son, "Billy, see that? Hell will look like that, only hell will be worse."

The storm was viewed as punishment, too. More than 100 people were some miles outside Tyrone (Oklahoma) on that Sunday afternoon, engaged in a rabbit drive that was expected to rid the neighborhood of 50,000 of the pests. Not so.

The black cloud struck just as the rabbits were being forced into the corner for the kill. Someone reported all but about 1500 rabbits escaped in the total blackness. Later a woman told the organizer of the rabbit drive that it was God's punishment for having a rabbit drive on the Sabbath. And one participant in that drive said there was never again one on Sunday, at least not that year.

And just how thick was this "granddaddy of 'em all"? Well, it was "so thick you could stick your finger in it and make a hole." "It was so thick prairie dogs dug their holes *up*." "It was so thick Lady Godiva could ride through the streets without even her horse seeing her."

And just how fine was this dust? Well, it was "like black

flour" or "the ashes of hell" and it was so fine that "it half filled a five-gallon jug with the cork still in it."

Just how black was this blackest of dusters? "Black as carbon black," "black as Carlsbad Cavern when they turn the lights out," "black as an angus bull," "black as the inside of a whale's belly at midnight," and "three midnights in a jug were bright compared to that dark."

What did it look like as it rushed down toward the south? It looked like "a carpet unrolling—a *big* carpet unrolling *fast*," "like a headrise on a creek," "like a rolling, boiling oil field fire," "like a horizontal tornado," "like it was on wheels," "like big ol' ocean waves just a-rollin'," "like Armageddon was right on top of us."

A young man newly married had been to Shawnee, Oklahoma, looking for a job—not an easy thing to find in 1935. Hitchhiking back toward Beaver, he was given a ride by a deputy sheriff, but the big black cloud enveloped them before they could get to Beaver, so the deputy dropped off his passenger at a friend's house to spend the night. After the young man got home the next morning, his wife asked him nothing about the storm or his being stranded away from home; she asked him if he'd found a job. And he had good news for her. Not everyone was more concerned about the storm than anything else.

Enterprising persons took advantage of the unique quality of the storm. They bottled the dust and sold it: "Genuine 1935 Rolling Duster Dust—25 cents." And something every Dust Bowl family needed the day after the great storm: "Dust Vacuum for Yards!" [*A newspaper ad.*]

### TURNSTILE: Memoir XXXV
By Thomas Thompson
(Amarillo Globe-Times, *Friday, October 9, 1970*)

During a dust storm in the '30s a traveler heading east stopped for gas in Bushland (Texas).

"What's the name of this desert?" he asked.

"This ain't no desert. That was a desert you just came through."

"Maybe so," said the stranger, "but there weren't any damned fools out there trying to raise wheat."

Not all dust storms were black. We had brown dust storms and yellow dust storms. Once we cleaned up after an off-white duster, but the first one was black, and the dust was as fine as pumice.

On a late Sunday afternoon I witnessed its approach while playing tennis on the Amarillo Tennis Club courts. The courts were at 33rd and Washington where a South Amarillo fire station now stands.

At first we thought it was a spring thunderstorm moving in from the north, and we continued our doubles game.

A player waiting in his car turned on his radio. He hollered, "Say, it's dust! It's black dust! In Dumas they can't see across the street!"

We stopped our game. I moistened my lips. The air was perfectly still and cloudless. The sky was blue. The sun shone down on that towering mountain of blackness.

"It's over the Canadian River," shouted the man listening to the car radio. "It will be hitting Pleasant Valley in another 10 minutes."

We were mesmerized. Deliberately we took down the nets, crawled in our cars and drove to our respective homes. I put my mother's car in the garage and closed and locked the overhead doors.

My mother was alone in the house waiting beside the radio. She had pulled down all the shades and assembled candles and coal oil lamps. She had cooked rice and a chicken dish and the pleasant odor pervaded the house.

"Somebody said the lights may go off," she said. "Are you hungry?"

"As a matter of fact, I am," I said.

We spent the evening listening to the radio warn listeners to stay indoors. Newscasters reported accidents and speculated on the cause of the phenomenon.

Before going to bed I asked my mother if she was sorry she had come to this God-forsaken country.

"Why should I be?" she finally said and closed her eyes. "Aubrey and I were happy here, and don't you say God-forsaken."

The next morning the sun was shining. The wind which had never really reached gale velocity had calmed.

A black, greasy dust covered the furniture. I opened the medicine cabinet. The dust was there. It was on the tube of toothpaste.

Before going to Wolflin School, I drove by a rent house a painter had finished over the weekend. It was dark adobe.

*The following verses that came out of the black storm and out of the Dust Bowl in general show something of the spirit of the people. The first is from the* Guymon Daily Herald, *Pioneer Edition, April 13–14, 1985. After discussing the '30s in general, Ralph Bennett closes his comments with this verse:*

### Black Duster

From out the bitter North the dust storm came,
Majestic in its might, unbowed by shame.
A myriad birds forgetting they could sing,
With startled trepidation took to wing.
A mighty curtain hung across the sky,
Billowing black, but streaked with gold and gray.
Inexorably it came and, towering high,
Threatened to blot the sun, and close the day.
The chickens went to roost. It seemed too soon
That night should come just shortly after noon.
Scurrying people into shelter fled;
And who could blame the man who bowed his head?
And who could ridicule the prayer he said?
The air was still. And then the monster struck!
With quivering force, like Nature run amok!
The light of day was blotted from the land
By tons of stifling dust and blistering sand!
No eyes could pierce that rushing ghastly gloom
Of tortured Spirits driven to their doom,
Protesting, screeching, but to no avail.
All day the storm raged on. Or was it night?
It seemed so long since earth had lost its light,
But by the morrow all the wind had fled;
Still in the sky the dust hung overhead;
And at the dawn the sun was old and red.

*The following verse deals with dust storms in general more than with the big black one of Palm Sunday, 1935. The author's comments about Black Sunday are in Chapter One.*

### Dirty-Thirty Days
By Betty Fisher Williams

There is a point in time—the kids want to know
What it was like to live in yester-year—long ago?
Especially do they seem to want to feel the effects
Of the so-called Dirty-30's—it leaves me perplexed!

Yes, it was bad, as the rains failed to water the land,
When the winds blew, either from the north or south made
  sand.
Sand came in the house, by the door, window, or roof—it laid
  everywhere;
We shook sand off the bed covers, wiped it off the table, eating
  with care.

On one particular spring day, it was Sunday; a church gathering
  was the setting.
A huge black cloud approached from the north, set us to fret-
  ting.
It almost seemed to us watching, like the end of the world,
As it swallowed us in darkness, for hours its fury unfurled.

We learned little tricks to try to survive with all our might.
Like herding the chickens into the henhouse; they, thinking it
  was night,
Would stay out in the fields—trying to roost, very
  unsafe . . .
All the animals confused—not knowing—was it early or late.

At times we tried to cover our face with masks,
But even after the wind and dirt settled, we had tasks:
To sweep the floors sent the dust flying into the air,
And it always resettled—after floating about—somewhere.

The topic of conversation, when visiting friends or neighbors,

And after a particular bad siege of wind and dirt,
Was sweeping up the mess, trying to dig out from under,
Each jokingly trying to out-do the others by announcing it in
  buckets-worth.

Somehow we clung to life, and hoped it someday would rain.
Yes, we coughed, but we learned to cope, happier days came.
There is still talk of the return of the so-called dirty 30's,
So here's one for the records—don't give up, it makes one
  sturdy.

But the wind and the sand did not always blow and go:
Life on the farm was both fun and interesting, with lots of
  chores to do.
Cows and horses must be cared for—herding cows took days
  and days.
Chickens must be fed and watered, eggs gathered, and pigs
  raised.

Then there was fun with brothers, sisters, neighbor kids and
  school;
We rode horses to school, except when we walked, games was
  the rule.
Even then we hurried home to help with the work, always something there.
Before TV and radio, no time to need entertainment, leisure
  time was rare.

Occasionally there were church socials, neighborhood get-to-
  gethers
And a community picnic at a lake or grove.
Then the older young people would find a chance
To sneak off into a thicket, to steal a kiss—ah, young love.

Now it is the 1980's and the joy of living in this day and age
Must be amplified by living as we knew life then at that stage.
If kids today could live the 1930's for a few months just to see
How exciting today's world is—to be alive—just take it from
  me. . . .

*This one-act play, "Dust," refers to the Black Blizzard only incidentally, though the storm does play a significant role in the drama.*

**Ben Guill's recollection of the writing of the play:**

"I was working in the oil field, back up roughnecking out here west of town. I had a friend that worked at the newspaper named Archer Fullingim, very able man. Wrote beautifully. And he and I were shooting the breeze one day and I said, 'You know, Arch, I'm going to write a play. I'm going to try. I'd like to.' He said, 'What's it going to be about?' I said, 'Would you collaborate with me? 'Cause you write well.' He said, 'Well, you go ahead and write what you want and let's see what we can do with it.' . . . The main thing was write about something I knew. I thought, 'Well, I'll just go ahead and write about that dust storm.' So I just started on it as something to do in the evenings. I wasn't dating. In the day time too, 'cause you'd work certain tours. It kind of evolved. Along about that time, in the dust storms they had dust pneumonia going around. . . . And people were losing their farms and ranches and so many things were going on. So I thought, 'Well, I think it should be a theme for a little play.' I'm very fond of one-act plays because I was coaching them in high school and the kids had done well."

Mr. Guill did finish the "little play," with the help of Mr. Fullingim, and he and his students (Dickie Kennedy, Arno Goddard, and Mary Adams) presented the play in the regional and state contests, where it won first place.

## DUST
### A Play in One Act
by
Ben Guill and Archer Fullingim

### A FOREWORD

This play is an insight into the life and hardships of the average ranch family in the great Southwest—a tribute to the pioneer spirit, which is still endowed in them—a picture of the spring of nineteen thirty-five anywhere in the Dust Bowl, fictionized, but which could have been, and was real to many.

## CHARACTERS

*John Anderson*—A man of 40 years, dependable, stolid and hard-working, but who is able to find in his wife a spirit that enables him to face overwhelming hardships.

*Sarah Anderson*—A daughter of pioneers. A mother and a good wife.

*Tom Anderson*—A twelve-year-old boy, who has been overcome by the dust. A typical ranch boy with his prize calf.

*Scene:* The home of a moderately well-to-do rancher. A combination of living, sleeping and dining room, because of weather conditions. Windows are covered with sheets in order to keep out as much dust as possible. The mother is busy cleaning house, and the boy is lying on a single bed. The wind is blowing and one can hear in the distance the bawling of thirsty and hungry cattle.

*Boy (speaking with difficulty).* Mother! Mother!

*Mother.* I'm coming, son. (*She sits by the side of the bed and begins to fan the boy.*) What is it? Tom?

*Boy.* Is . . . the dust getting worse?

*Mother.* There's only a dusty haze, Tom. The wind ain't blowin' very much now.

*Boy.* I can't breathe . . . It hurts!

*Mother (adjusting wet cloth on boy's face).* You mustn't talk son . . . and we'll keep this wet cloth over your mouth and nose . . . like this.

*Boy (removing cloth).* I wish it would stop.

*Mother.* It will soon. It's got to rain sometime. You must hush, now, and be quiet.

*Boy (gasping for breath as he speaks).* I—can't . . .

*Mother.* Hush, hush, Tom . . .

*Boy.* The wind . . . the dust . . .

*Mother.* Shh-h-h-h-h . . .

*Boy.* The cows . . . my little calf!

*Mother (realizing the need of his being quiet).* Sh-h-h-h-h. You must stop talking and rest. Just forget about it all.

(*The boy's efforts to talk cause him to go into a spasm of coughing and choking. The mother gives him medicine and covers his mouth and continues to fan him. The boy becomes quiet, and after a moment she rises and goes to the phone and rings.*)

*Mother (speaking loudly over the country telephone).* Hello—hello, central—ring Dr. Walker's office, please. *(pause)* Hello—hello—is this Dr. Walker's office? . . . Well, this is Mrs. Anderson. Is the doctor in? . . . *(disheartedly)* Where is he? . . . Yes . . . Is that so? . . . Oh, I'm so sorry. *(turns and looks at the boy and, with choked voice, repeats)* . . . Oh! Please tell him to come out to our place as soon as he can. It's Tom . . . he's worse . . . tell him to come down the highway to Lively's place and Mr. Lively will let him have a horse to carry him over here. The sand drifts on the east and west road are too deep for a car . . .

*Boy (restless because of the mother's loud talking, calls).* Mother!

*Mother (turns and looks at the boy and then continues, hurriedly)* . . . They've filled the bar pits and have completely covered the fences . . .

*Boy (weakly).* Mother!

*Mother.* . . . I sure do thank you and please tell the doctor to hurry. Goodbye. *(Rings off and hurries to the bedside and begins to fan the boy.)* I'm coming.

*Father (entering and closing door quickly behind him, comes to the foot of the bed and in a hushed, sick-room voice, he speaks).* Sarah . . .

*(The mother raises her hand for him to be quiet. He stands for a moment looking at his son, then goes slowly to the washstand. He removes his hat and jacket, rinses his mouth and washes his face and hands. Picking up the towel, he turns and comes back to the center of the stage. The mother, seeing that the boy is asleep, puts down her fan and walks slowly to meet her husband.)*

*Father (softly).* How is the boy, Sarah?

*Mother.* He talked "right smart" a few minutes ago, but I believe he's getting worse. He has a hurting in his chest . . . it seems hard for him to breathe and he had a spell of coughing and choking. I called the doctor but his office girl says that he's been out on calls night and day . . . thirty cases of dust pneumonia . . . but she said he might could get out here this evening . . . And John . . . Mrs. Power's little girl died this morning. *(She turns and goes to the bed. He goes to the wash stand and slowly hangs up his towel and, turning front, he bitterly speaks.)*

*Father.* We're all gonna die if we don't get out of here. *(He walks slowly toward the bed.)* Everything and everybody . . . Sarah . . . Tom . . . he . . . looks . . .

*Mother (moving quickly to her husband, and, almost hysterically).*
No! . . . John . . . don't say it . . . *(a slight sob).*
   *Father (taking her in his arms—realizing his speech has hurt her).*
I'm sorry, Sarah . . . I'm sorry . . . but this dust is enough to kill
anybody.
   *Mother (looks at him and speaks with a choked voice).* I know it's
bad, John . . . but it can't go on like this forever.
   *Father.* I hope it can't. We can't even live decent. There's so
much dirt that we got to eat and sleep in one room so's you can
keep things halfway clean.
   *Mother (bravely).* But I don't mind . . . John . . . I don't mind.
*(She looks at boy, and as if she were praying.)* I . . . I . . . just hope. . . .
Oh, how I hope our boy gets well again! *(She turns back to her husband.)* And we can save our cattle and our land. *(Then, bravely)*
Did you try to list the north field to keep it from blowing?
   *Father (discouragingly).* No . . . I quit . . . It won't do no good
. . . The top soil is pret-near gone. Four to six inches already
blowed away . . . If it keeps on it'll be so no account it won't grow
nothin'. The tank is bone dry . . . I tried to build a trough to
catch what water the windmill is pumping, but the dust almost
blots it up before the cattle can get what little there is. They're
suffering . . . have been for weeks . . . Listen to 'em. *(Sarah follows him and they both stand listening to the bawling of the cattle.)*
Listen to 'em, Sarah . . . I can't stand it no longer. *(Turns and
grasps her hands, then, pleadingly)* We've got to leave here, Sarah.
   *Mother (leading him downstage and speaking to him as if he were
a child).* We can't leave now, John. Why, this is all we've got. We've
been here twelve long years . . . some of them have been awful
hard . . . this is worse, I know . . . but this place is ours. It'll rain
soon . . . I know it will.
   *Father (slowly).* Twelve years . . . twelve years . . . it's been a
long time of hard work for both of us . . . and now it's all gone
. . . our boy . . . maybe . . . dying. Everything dying—or dead.
Rain . . . it ain't rained for two years . . . it can't rain. *(Gradually
raising his voice)* It's blown dust for four solid months . . . the air's
all filled with it . . . clouds of dust . . . we eat it . . . we breathe it
. . .it even shuts out the sun. *(Loudly)* There ain't enough water
in a hundred miles to stop the cattle from bawlin' . . . we ain't
raised enough grain in two years to feed one cow!

*Boy (awakes and calls).* Mother!

*Mother.* Hush, John. *(Goes quickly to the boy.)*

*Father (lowering his voice).* Much less the few head we got left. Sarah, most of 'em are down and can't get up!

*Mother (after quieting the boy, she comes quickly back to her husband).* But the government is going to help us, John . . . lend us the money to buy feed . . . and show us how to save the cattle and the land.

*Father.* The government . . . they can't . . . the cattle are too far gone . . . and they can't put the top soil back on the land. Nobody can help us. Why, the doctor can't even get out here to see our sick boy. *(The boy chokes and gasps. The parents go to the bed.)*

*Boy.* Papa! Papa! *(Mother gives him a drink and he rests.)*

*Father (gently and quickly).* What is it, son?

*Boy (slowly and with difficulty).* Can't you stop the cattle from bawling? . . . Why don't you feed and water them? . . . I can hear my little calf . . . please don't let him suffer . . . he wants water . . . and remember . . . you said we would take him to the stock show . . . remember? . . . you promised . . .

*Father.* Yes, I remember. We're going to take him. You'll be well and strong by then. Quiet, now. *(The boy begins to sleep; they sit by the bed watching with worried, haggard faces. The father rises and goes to a rocking chair and sits. He rocks slowly. His wife comes and stands beside him.)*

*Mother (visualizing the past).* John, you've only been out here about thirteen years . . . I've been here all my life . . . I've seen other hard times and Mama used to tell me of the terrible times she and Papa used to have. They came west in a covered wagon—it took them almost two months to make the trip—and when they finally settled, they had to live in a dugout. Then Indians would raid them and run off all the stock. Papa was nearly killed in one of those raids. Once the locusts came over in such numbers the sun was hidden. They ate every blade of grass in a strip two miles wide. Prairie fires burnt out the ranch twice, wiping out every living thing. Then the drought in the eighties lasted nearly three years. Mama said they almost starved to death, but they wouldn't leave. . . . We do have enough to eat . . . so you see, John, we can't give up.

*Father (explaining).* Sarah, they were ranchers. They didn't try to raise no crops. The drought won't last forever, because I figger it'll rain sometime. We shouldn't never plowed up this land. It was the sod that kept it from blowing . . . but cattle have been so cheap, we couldn't make a livin' out of 'em. We had to try farming.

*Mother.* I know . . . I know.

*Father.* If it don't rain soon we're gonna have to leave, and if we have another bad dust storm, the cattle will choke to death, and Tom won't pull through.

*Mother (goes to the bed, leans over and touches the boy's forehead; she draws her hand quickly back and in a frightened voice).* John! his fever's awful high . . . I'm . . . going to call the doctor again. *(Goes to the phone and rings.)* Hello, central . . . ring Dr. Walker's office again, please. *(pause)* Hello . . . hello *(relief in her voice)*, Dr. Walker . . . this is Mrs. Anderson. Tom's worse and we want you to come to our place right away . . . What? . . . Oh . . . thank you . . . doctor *(she slowly replaces the receiver and bows her head against the phone).*

*Father (turning at the sound of despair in her voice, he waits for her to finish and fearfully asks).* What is it? What's wrong now?

*Mother (turning and speaking slowly and with despair).* John . . . he can't come . . . a dust storm has hit town and turned daylight into pitch black darkness. It's . . . so thick he can't see to drive his car . . . even with the lights on. He says . . . to prepare for it . . . because it's coming this way. *(They both turn and look at the boy. John goes quickly to the door as Sarah comes and stands by the boy's bed.)*

*Father.* My God! . . . All the dust in the world is piled up in that thing! . . . Come look at it, Sarah.

*Mother (joins him and at the sight that meets her eyes, turns and whispers fearfully).* John . . .

*Father.* It's traveling fast . . . the cattle know it's coming . . . Listen to 'em, Sarah . . . They know it's coming. *(They stand silently, listening. He suddenly turns, goes to the corner of the room and gets his rifle, holds it for a moment, and looks at the boy. Sarah turns and stares at her husband . . . a realization of what he is about to do fixes itself in her mind.)*

*Mother (fearfully).* John! . . . What are you going to do?

*Father (walking toward the door).* I'm going to put those cattle out of their misery.

*Mother (trying to stop him).* They might pull through! They might not die! *(He pulls away from her and leaves. She stands in the door gazing after him, hysterically calling.)* No! John! . . . Don't! *(There is a shot and she leans against the door facing, resting her head on her arms. There is another shot.)*

*Boy (becomes conscious of the shots and calls).* Mother! What's that? *(She hurriedly closes the door, wipes the tears from her eyes and goes to him.)* Someone is shooting . . . *(another shot)* . . . they might kill my little calf!

*Mother.* No, son . . . it's your father. *(There is another shot and the only sound is the bawling of one calf—the boy's calf. There is a pause and one final shot and all is quiet.)*

*Boy.* Mother . . . my calf has quit bawling . . . did Papa water him? He won't let him suffer any more?

*Mother (a sob in her voice but relief at his last question).* No, son . . . he won't let him suffer any more.

*(John returns and puts up the rifle. He looks at the boy and then at the mother, bows his head and turns away. He removes the sheet from the window, takes it to the wash stand and rewets it, returns and replaces it over the window. Sarah goes and gets the cloth for the boy's face. After a few moments, she joins her husband who is standing at the door watching the approaching storm.)*

*Father (speaking with an awe-inspired voice and visualizing the horror of the approaching storm).* It don't look like dust. It looks like smoke . . . a rolling, blowing wall of black smoke . . . a mile high . . . and it stretches as far as you can see. That wall is gonna fall on us, Sarah . . . look . . . the birds that are flying in front of it. They seem to realize that it means death.

*Mother (impressed by the terrifying spectacle).* It's beautiful . . . John . . . terribly beautiful . . . no one in the west has ever seen anything like it before. *(Turns to the boy.)* If only it didn't cause so much suffering. *(She returns and sits on the downstage side of the bed. John comes from the door . . . looks to see if everything is all right, and sits on the upstage side of the bed. Sarah leans over and kisses the boy and as she raises up, the duster hits. They look at one another and glance toward the outside, terrified at the startling suddenness and blackness of the storm.)*

*Mother (her voice a frightened whisper).* No wonder the doctor couldn't come . . . It's as black as night . . . I wonder why the wind ain't blowing.

*Father.* It'll be here soon . . . It's got all this dust piled up in front of it.

*Mother.* John . . . this scares me. Do you suppose that this is the end of everything?

*Father.* I . . . I . . . don't know, Sarah. *(The sand begins to patter on the house. It sounds like rain, and the wind begins to blow. The boy grows restless and begins to struggle for breath as the air becomes filled with dust.)*

*Boy (choking and gasping).* It's . . . raining . . . I can hear it. *(Struggles for breath)* I . . . can't . . . breathe . . .

*Mother (swiftly fanning the boy).* John, light the lamp! Hurry! *(John gropes across the room, lights the lamp as his wife calls again.)* Hurry, John! *(He brings the lamp and places it on the chair by the bed. He sinks to his knees.)* John, the medicine!

*Father (gives medicine to the boy).* I'll fan him, Sarah. You keep the wet cloth on his face. *(The boy struggles for breath and fights the cloth.)*

*Mother (frantically).* John! He's choking to death . . . can't . . . we do . . . something?

*Father.* Raise up his head, Sarah. *(She does so. He doubles the pillow and puts it under the boy's head.)*

*Mother (whispering).* John . . . I believe . . . he's dying! *(They both work with the boy as the death rattle becomes more audible. Finally, a deep breath and the child dies. John slowly stops fanning, and Sarah leans over and listens . . . she raises her head and speaks fearfully.)* My baby! . . . John! . . . he's stopped breathing! He's stopped breathing, John! He's . . . he's . . . dead! *(She begins to cry, leans over and takes the child in her arms. John, who has watched her with a dazed expression on his face, bows his head over both of them, his body racked by hard, dry sobs. After a moment he rises, picks up the lamp, stands looking at Sarah and Tom, and slowly turns and stumbles across, sets the lamp on the table, turns toward Sarah, and speaks, brokenly.)*

*Father.* We've got to leave here . . . *(his voice rises hysterically)* we've got to leave . . . who wants to stay in this dry, dusty desert hole? . . . where nothing can live . . . years of work wiped out in a few months . . . Sarah, we can't stay no longer. There's nothing left for us. The land gone . . . the cattle gone . . . and now . . .

we . . . we've lost our boy. *(He sinks into a chair, his head in his arms . . . crying . . . thoroughly broken. At the beginning of his hysteria, Sarah rises from the bed and turns to him, realizing his need for her. She turns to the bed and covers the face of the child. As she does so, she also breaks, but she recovers and goes to John and kneels by his chair.)*

*Mother (brokenly).* We can't leave now, John . . . we can't leave now. *(Raising her head, she prays.)* Oh, God . . . let it rain . . . don't let other people suffer like we've suffered. *(At the finish of her prayer, she bows her head and they both grow quiet. John puts his arms about her shoulders. After a moment, she raises her head, her face shining with the hope and courage that her prayer has given her, and she continues.)* I wish . . . oh . . . How I wish he could have lived to see it rain!

*(John, too, raises his head as he seems able to find in this pioneer woman the sustained courage to carry on.)*

CURTAIN

*There is little doubt that many Dust Bowl people were afflicted by having to breathe the dust that was everywhere in the air almost all the time— not merely in 1935 but for much of the time through the early to late 1930s. "Dust pneumonia," however, was probably more an irritant to the lungs than it was a disease, in the usual sense of that word. Dr. R. M. Bellamy, a physician in Pampa, Texas, during the 1930s, when asked what he thought dust pneumonia was, replied: "Well, I know that, in my opinion, what it was was . . . of course, we all have bacteria in our respiratory tract. And when anything comes along to lower the resistance, any irritant—and that's what it was, an irritant—it wasn't that the pneumonia germs floated in with this dirt. The pneumonia germs were already there. But our immunity took care of it, you know. But when you got the irritation—the mechanical irritation of this dust—that's my opinion. I don't remember having any cases of it. It was a mixed infection of the bugs that we always have in the lungs. I never read anybody proving that there was any different germ. Don't think it was that. I think it was a mechanical irritation on top of normal bacteria flora that's normally present."*

*Nevertheless, much distress was probably dealt to people who were outdoors much: farmers, especially, who had to plow and harrow on windy days (as well as the infrequent calm ones), and when the wind blew in those years, it picked up dust almost everywhere in that region of the country.*

# EPILOGUE

The Great Dust Storm of April, 14, 1935, the most widely remembered of the hundreds of storms that raced through the plains states during the 1930s, was not the same kind of natural disaster usually associated with memories, such as Hurricane Andrew, which nearly wiped part of southern Florida off the map; California earthquakes that often have shaken buildings, houses, and highways within their reach; volcanic eruptions, such as that of Mount Saint Helens, which left square miles shorn of all living things; floods that have forced whole cities to be abandoned and rebuilt on higher ground.

No, the Great Dust Storm on Black Sunday came in quietly, engulfed towns and cities in impenetrable darkness, then moved on southward, leaving almost everything as it had been the day before—except, of course, for the dust that had settled on everything in its path, including the insides of house and cars, and the eyes, ears, noses, and mouths of those who were caught outdoors.

According to literature about the storm, hardly any people were killed by the storm, though some probably had trouble breathing for a while. Hardly any property was destroyed, though the amount of dust blown in would have provided enough fertile soil to grow grain to feed the whole nation. Because the storm occurred during the worst times of the Great Depression, when people were worried about much more than storms, and because there was more dust blowing that spring than ever before or after, it is quite surprising that so many people, even those who were children when the storm came through, carry vivid impressions of the event. The reminiscences

151

in this study demonstrate that it was an incredibly different kind of storm from those that preceded it and those that followed. Some who remember this storm even maintain that it was not the worst storm of the Dust Bowl era, only the most unusual.

Furthermore, the storm is still newsworthy from time to time, even celebrated in newspapers and magazines fifty years afterward.

Partly because the storm did not come the typical way of most dust storms—in howling wind that whipped the dirt out of the ground and thrust it into the air and across the prairies—and partly because it came during a day that had been warm and beautiful after two months of almost constant wind and dust, the Black Sunday storm rolled in from the far north, gathering momentum in a cold front, and darkened instantly every activity in which people were engaged that day. It was frightening, beautiful—a different kind of storm. So different that it remains fresh in the memories of those who experienced it.